The desire to use collected items and natural dyeing techniques in art is part of a growing movement to be more sustainable and more mindful of how we live – how we connect with one another and the places we live in. More and more textile artists are using natural processes in their work, from dyeing with rust to working with found and scavenged items, and this book is the first to bring these increasingly popular techniques together. It promotes a way of working creatively with what is close at hand, whether gathered on walks by the seashore or collected in your garden, and working in tune with natural processes, bringing the rhythms and unpredictability of nature into your work.

Examples of this type of working include using local plants – such as blackberries, dandelions and, in the case of one Australian contributor, eucalyptus leaves – along with found metals to eco-dye fabrics and threads. Use rust to make marks and prints on cloth and paper, which can then be further stitched and layered. Foraged items – such as nettles, driftwood, scrap metal or acorns – can be weaved, stitched into or incorporated into tapestry. Finally there is advice on combining all the techniques to create stunning textural work that is a comment on, and a product of, its surroundings.

The book is illustrated with the finest examples of contemporary embroidery and textile-art work using nature, by artists whose practice is tied up with their experience of and respect for the natural environment. It captures a very strong sense of place and a feeling of calm.

Natural
Processes
in Textile Art

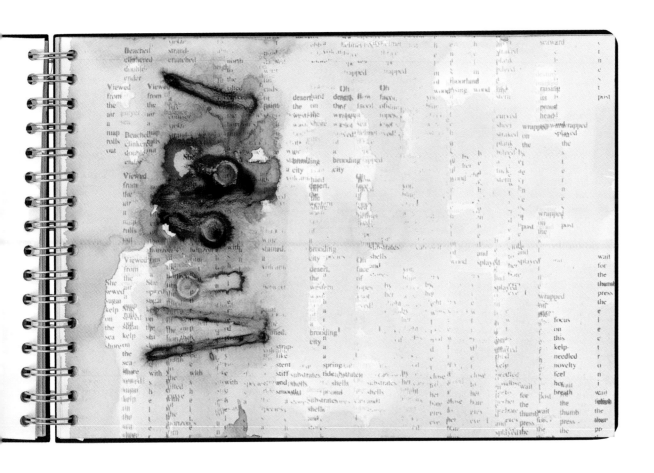

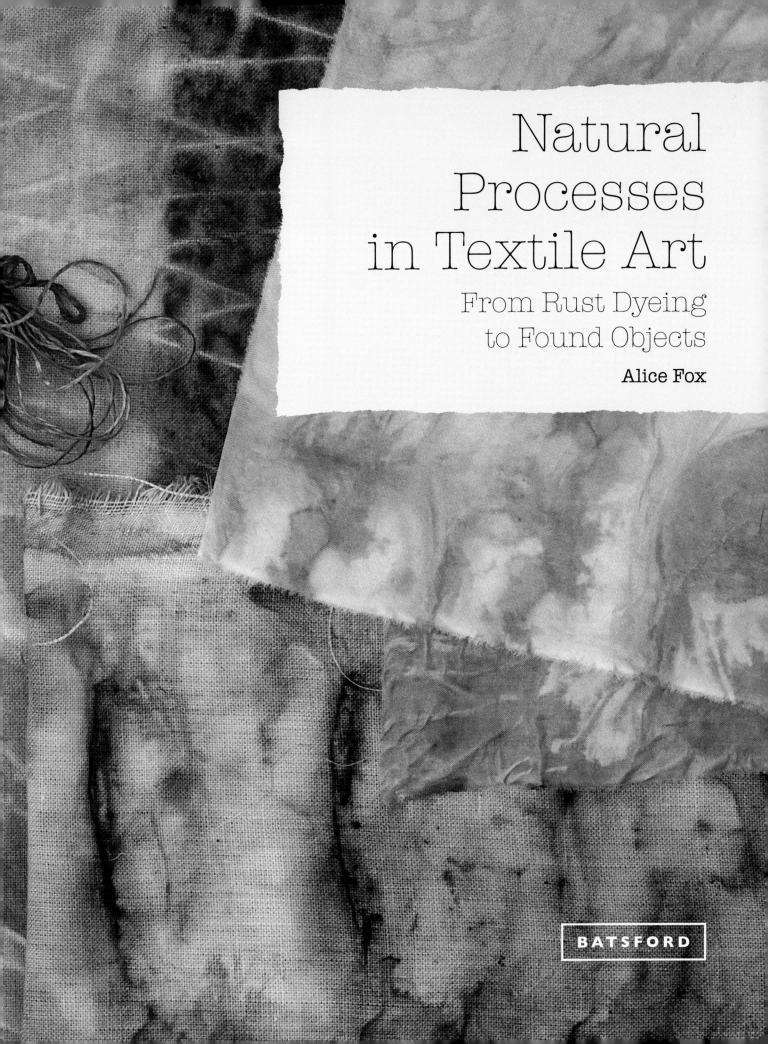

Natural Processes in Textile Art

From Rust Dyeing to Found Objects

Alice Fox

BATSFORD

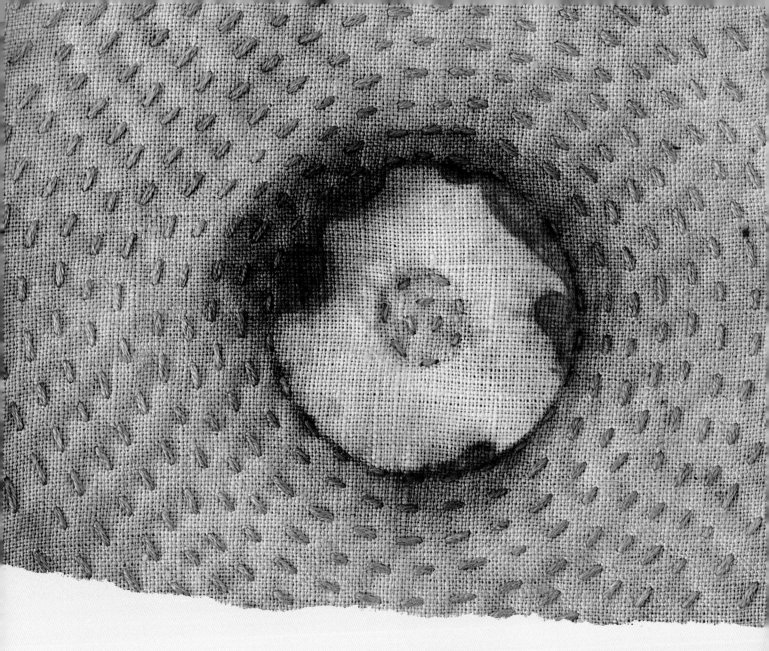

First published in the United Kingdom in 2015 by
Batsford
1 Gower Street
London WC1E 6HD

An imprint of Pavilion Books Company Ltd

ISBN: 9781849942980

A CIP catalogue record for this book is available from the
British Library.

20 19 18 17 16
10 9 8 7 6 5 4 3 2

Reproduction by Rival Colour Ltd, UK
Printed and bound by Craft Print Holding Pte Ltd, Singapore

This book can be ordered direct from the publisher at the
website: www.pavilionbooks.com, or try your local bookshop.

Distributed in the United States and Canada
by Sterling Publishing Co., Inc.1166 Avenue of the Americas,
17th Floor, New York, NY 10036

Contents

Introduction

This book gathers together a range of techniques in textile art that make use of natural processes. It promotes a way of working creatively with what is easily available or close at hand, around the home and further afield. The aim is to be imaginative with what can be gathered from your surroundings and make work that is in tune with the natural world. We will explore a variety of ways to make use of found, foraged or scavenged items.

The desire to use collected items and natural dyeing techniques in art is part of a growing movement to be more sustainable. We will discuss ways of working with nature, appreciate 'slow' processes and look for ways of capturing the unpredictability of nature.

The book features the work of artists whose practice is tied up with their experience of, and respect for, the natural environment. They often capture a sense of place through their work.

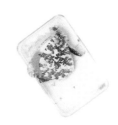

Wild beginnings

I have always had a strong relationship with the natural world. Even as a child, environmental issues were important to me and I felt that everything should be done in a sensitive way with respect for resources and future generations. I was fascinated by natural history and was an avid collector of found things: dead beetles or butterflies, feathers, leaves and birds' skulls. I still have many of them.

Footprints and the marks made by wildlife were a source of interest and I keenly looked them up in identification books and catalogued what I'd seen. I also loved to draw my finds and I would pore over books of natural-history illustration. My interests in the arts and natural sciences were well balanced but initially I chose to go down the science route, completed a degree in physical geography and had a short career in nature conservation. Both reinforced my understanding of how the world around us works and increased my appreciation of the fragility of ecosystems and landscapes.

Now, as a professional artist, my artistic practice has a strong link to the natural world and strives to take the environment into account. The use of natural processes is a key part of it.

Above and opposite: A personal collection of natural found objects, used for study and inspiration.

Influential art

I have long been inspired by the work of artists who have a strong connection to the natural world, in particular Andy Goldsworthy, Richard Long, Chris Drury and David Nash. These artists work directly with nature, often making artworks that are ephemeral or subject to change through their exposure to the elements. Some of their works are made through the action of their bodies in the landscape and some are fleeting moments recorded in photographs, the resulting image becoming the work of art. These artists work mostly with natural materials, often gathered from the landscape. This appeals to me both aesthetically and idealistically.

The exploration of different and sometimes unconventional materials fascinates me. It is only through working with a particular material that you come to know it and its potential. I see this as a means of understanding the world around me. Artist Sue Lawty's contemplative work is very much about engagement with the landscape on different levels, and her exploration of different materials pushes the boundaries of tapestry weaving and textile art. I was fortunate to spend time helping in her studio whilst I was a student, and it was a formative experience.

Above and right: Sycamore keys, gathered while walking, can be embroidered with simple hand stitch.

In my work I employ techniques from a wide range of areas including textiles, fine art printmaking and tapestry weaving. I build up layers of print and stitch, working on the surface of paper or cloth. I use the word 'print' to cover a wide range of mark-making techniques. Some of these marks are made by dyeing or staining and are fairly uncontrollable. Some are much more precise. Texture is as important as the marks, and layers of print and stitch change the texture of the surface I am working on. Detail is also important. My work is often referred to as subtle; if you look closely, there is a lot going on. I work fairly interchangeably with cloth and paper, treating the latter as a type of textile and recognizing that each material I work with has its own properties and potential.

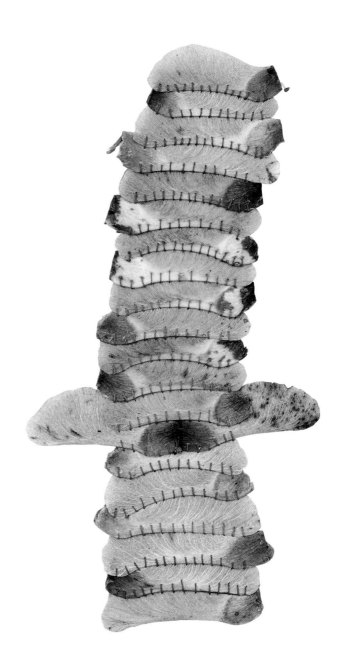

Balancing act

I see everyday life and my artistic practice as a continuum. They are interrelated and sometimes impossible to unpick from one another. In many ways this is born of necessity: a busy family life caring for children and balancing this with work and hobbies makes for small parcels of time available for creative pursuits. Half an hour here or an hour there, snatched between other commitments is sometimes all there is. I have developed ways of making use of these moments. My textiles degree was completed part-time as a mature student with small children.

It is important to make the most of any time available. I will often be thinking through ideas for things I want to experiment with whilst doing household tasks that don't require much concentration or detailed decision-making, such as doing the washing-up, cooking a meal or hanging out the washing. This means that when I do get to my desk or studio, I usually know exactly what I shall do first or have a list of things I want to try.

Influences can come from all areas of your everyday life. The things that I see on a journey to the post office or on the school run feed into what I do in the studio just as much as the experience of walking on a remote beach hundreds of miles away from home. It is the experience of whatever landscape I am in that counts, being present in the moment and taking notice of the detail of what is around me. There may not always be time to record these small observations straight away. But making a mental note takes no time and these thoughts can be cumulative – the more you notice, the more you have to draw on when there is time to devote to creativity. Keep a small notebook or sketchbook to hand and you can usually scribble down a thought or observation, even if time is tight.

Right: *Tide Marks Book #49* (2013), 210 x 16cm (82½ x 6¼in). This artist's book is made from paper, rust print, collagraph print (using found objects) and hand stitch.

Green and slow

In recent years, 'green issues' have become mainstream and people increasingly make an effort to consider the environment in their everyday lives. The desire to use collected items and natural dyeing techniques in art is part of a growing movement to be more sustainable. Ideas are borrowed from the 'make do and mend' culture but new twists are given to old techniques. Many artists incorporate collected items, either natural or man-made, as a means of commenting on our interaction with, and impact on, the natural world. Some artists have chosen to use rubbish as a record of, or interpretation of, human impact. At a time of environmental change and uncertainty, artists can offer insight and new perspectives on the world around us, as well as a celebration of it.

There is an increasing awareness of the value of 'slow' processes, which foster an appreciation of responsible sourcing and mindfulness. The Slow Movement started in connection with food but has grown to embrace different aspects of how we live and connect with one another and with the places we live in.

Techniques

In harmony with the principles described on pages 10 and 11, this book provides ideas and examples of how natural processes can be used to achieve beautiful results in textile art. There is definitely an emphasis on the experimental. The beauty of many of the techniques we will be looking at is that they are unpredictable. I love that serendipitous aspect to the processes I use. There is a kind of magic to it all: something new to discover all the time. I want to celebrate that unpredictability, just as my work celebrates the uniqueness of each experience of the natural world.

Many of the techniques we will look at use found items. For me, these are a tangible link to the places I've been. However insignificant an item may seem to others, its inherent value to me is derived from the fact that I have come across it whilst walking, decided to pick it up and have used it as a way of recording the experience of that place. Often these will be natural items, things collected responsibly on walks (or items readily available around the home and garden). There is also a place for found man-made objects, particularly rusty metal. Using rust in conjunction with natural dyeing techniques has become a key element in my own work, initially through its availability on the particular beaches that have formed my focus in recent years. By exploring the possibilities of rust for printing, dyeing and mark-making, I have developed techniques that I can combine with other, more conventional ones, to give the visual and tactile effects I am after.

The potential for metal to provide and affect colour has relevance in natural dyeing. Metals often perform the role of a mordant, helping the plant-based colour to attach to the fibres being dyed. Natural dyeing is a specialist area of its own and we will only touch on certain dyeing techniques in this book. This will include methods for making marks on both paper and cloth.

I hope that by bringing techniques together that make use of what is readily available in your own environment (at home or in the places you visit) you will be inspired to use natural processes in your creative projects. Often the key to these techniques is time: taking time to see what is around you, to appreciate what is there and then allowing beautiful images and marks the time to develop naturally.

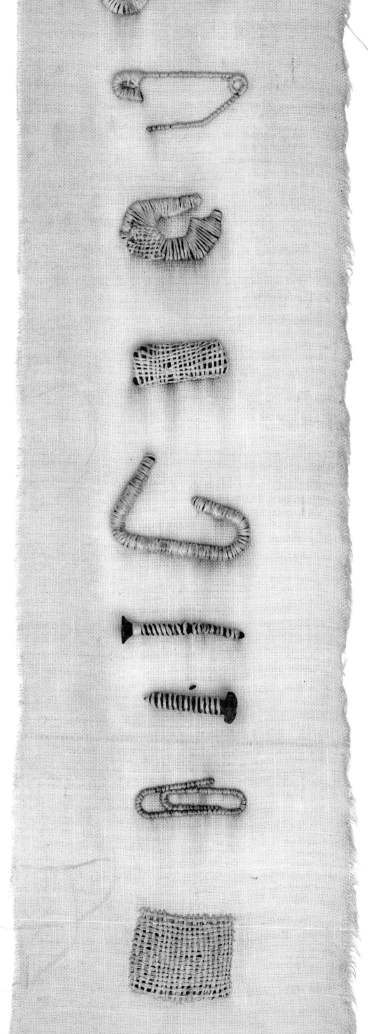

Right: Detail from *Rust Diary #2* (2014), 10 x 115cm (4 x 45¼in). Rusty found objects were hand stitched into linen and left out in the elements to stain slowly.

Using this book

This book is intended to be a source of inspiration and ideas. Often, I will be giving you a starting point in the hope that you will discover things that fascinate you. It is only through trying things out that you'll really learn what works for you. Be encouraged to explore and then take things in your own direction.

All the techniques can be used with minimal equipment: I try to keep things as low-tech and simple as possible. Everything should be achievable while out and about or on the kitchen table with basic materials.

You need to log possibilities. I use sketchbooks to record things I see while I'm out or for developing visual ideas for specific projects. I always have a small one of these in my bag. I have a notebook in which I put ideas about things I might try or develop. This contains sketches or diagrams, references to things I've seen or exhibitions I've visited.

I also have notebooks in which I keep a record of specific methods or techniques. This becomes really important when trying out new things, especially ones that you might want to repeat. Get into the habit of writing everything down and then you will always be able to refer back if you want to. Sometimes such technical notes are more usefully attached to samples, in which case I write them on a piece of paper to pin or clip to the sample or to slip into an envelope or ring-binder pocket.

Many examples of ways in which I've used the techniques are included in the book. Of course this is a very personal take. I have also selected a number of artists whose work I admire: their work illustrates how techniques might be employed in different ways. At the end of the book you'll find suggestions for further reading and resources. Most of all, it is important to enjoy what you do and feel right about how your creativity is realized – happy exploring.

Above: Sketchbooks, incorporating drawings made on walks, notes from exhibitions and found items.

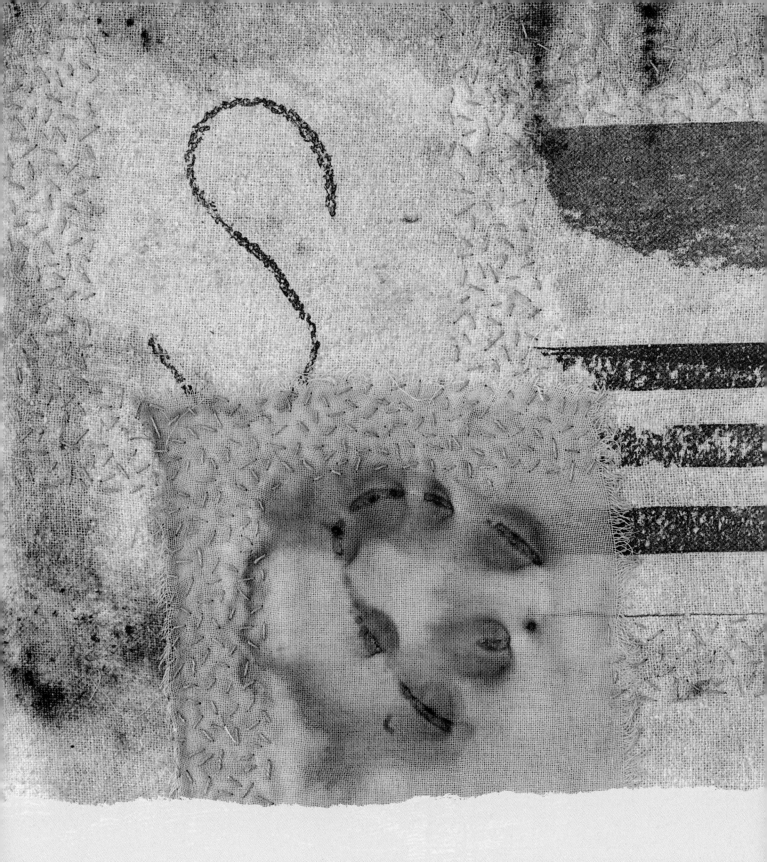

Above: Detail from *Pavement Piece #33* (2013), 35 x 24cm (13¾ x 9½in). Silk, cotton, rust print, collagraph print and selective hand stitch.

Chapter 1

Exploring, finding, collecting

Hunting and gathering

There are numerous possibilities for gathering materials that can be used for the various techniques described in this book. A walk in the woods, a rummage in the garden shed, even a quick walk to the local corner shop can throw up possibilities. Sometimes I will go out specifically to collect things – perhaps acorns or interesting leaves for eco printing. On other occasions it is a case of seeing what I find and being opportunistic. I tend to apply the mindset of a beachcomber to most places I go. You will be surprised at what is out there for the magpie creative scavenger.

Having always had a propensity to pick up items of interest I now find myself doing it almost unconsciously. I rarely return home without the odd leaf or rusty washer having found its way into my bag. But I am selective: things either need to have interest in terms of their form and feel (a newly fallen acorn has the most beautiful smooth, waxy surface) or have potential for making a mark through one process or another. Small metal objects (washers for example, or squashed beer-bottle tops) are particularly prized. I invariably have a small selection of these accumulating in my jacket pocket.

Left: Hand-woven sample using beach-combed rope and fabric.

Jilly Edwards

Journeys, walks and visits can be recorded and interpreted through sketchbooks, collecting objects and mark-making. A desire to capture the essence of a place is often what drives this process (see Chapter 6, page 112). For tapestry weaver Jilly Edwards, journeys are a recurring theme in her work. She often makes use of items collected on her travels, incorporating them into her unconventionally presented woven pieces. Her inspiration comes from the journey as well as the destination.

Artist's statement

'Often it's impossible to draw as you travel so I collect anything that interests me. The tickets became a mobile sketchbook. I ran out of sketchbooks on one long journey and the only thing I had to work on was my series of tickets from that journey. I made sure I retained the current ticket! Then I worked on the rest: covering, sticking things on, then drawing over them when I returned to my studio, where I also stitched over them. I was doing a rail trip every week for a year in which I acquired eight tickets each trip, so every week I used them to hold memories of the journeys.'

Above: Detail from *Travelling Sampler* (2010) by Jilly Edwards. Found objects, weave, stitch, text, paint and collage.

Botanical collecting

Plant material can be used for printing. This could be contact or eco printing (see Chapter 2, page 30), or direct printing using inks or paints (see Chapter 5, page 92). I aim only to collect leaves that have already fallen, either in a wild setting or on the street. In your own garden, or those you have permission to forage in, it is up to you to make your own rules. It could be really interesting to use the plants in your garden to make a record of the seasons or how things change over time. This would enhance the relationship that you already have with your little patch of land (even if it is only a window box!).

If you are collecting plant material that isn't to be used straight away, it needs to be stored in a way that allows air to circulate, to prevent it turning into a mouldy mess. Leaves are best pressed between paper with a weight on top (a newspaper or an old magazine is fine, with a couple of books on top). Seeds, twigs or other items can be stored in paper or fabric bags, which you could make from old scraps or rags.

Responsible collecting

It is important to be aware of the legal protection given to plants. In the UK and the Republic of Ireland it is illegal to uproot any wild plant without permission from the landowner or occupier. In protected areas such as nature reserves, Ministry of Defence or National Trust property, it is illegal to pick, uproot or remove plants. Note that even on a nature reserve, the removal of fallen leaves or berries isn't normally allowed. Certain rare plants have protection, making it illegal to pick, collect or cut them. In unprotected areas, picking is acceptable if done responsibly for personal use.

Guidelines for picking

- Only take flowers, leaves and berries from plants that are common and which you can identify.
- Always pick in moderation so that plenty remains for others to enjoy (bear in mind that the once-accepted guideline of taking no more than 10 per cent may be out of date now as more and more people collect).
- Be careful not to damage other vegetation when picking the plant you want.
- Always gain permission from the landowner.
- If you are abroad, familiarize yourself with the nature protection laws of the host country.

Left: Plant material gathered from local woodland.

Foraging hotspots

Coast

Beachcombing is an activity that most of us have engaged in at some point, whether purposefully or just picking up the odd pebble or shell as we walk. The constant supply of items thrown up by the tides means that there are always new possibilities. Some beaches collect more debris than others and there are websites that list particularly rich locations. There is often more debris on beaches after winter storms and before they have been cleaned up for the summer season.

The amount of rubbish on some beaches can be shocking; in parts of the world, a large part of the beach material is now made up of plastic debris. I find the mixture of natural and man-made debris fascinating and depressing in equal measure. Sometimes the two are so intermingled that it is difficult to identify which is which. The sea treats everything in exactly the same way and plastics just get broken into ever smaller pieces. If you are interested in tackling the rubbish problem, some local wildlife trusts and the Marine Conservation Society organize beach-cleaning events (see page 127).

Scour the beach for items that might be of use for printing, weaving and sewing. Charred wood can be used to draw or make marks. Feathers and sticks also make useful drawing tools, either on the beach or back in the studio. Collect the exquisite forms of sea urchins, shells or pebbles washed clean by the sea for inspiration and study.

Countryside

The countryside, whether consisting of managed or wild landscape, provides many opportunities for gathering plant material (see Guidelines for Picking, page 21). Twigs, leaves and seeds are obvious things to collect. Hedgerows have bountiful supplies of berries and seeds in the autumn. You might consider using some of these 'in the field' to draw with (see Chapter 2, page 54, for more ideas on this). Earth or mud can be used for mark-making or for staining cloth or paper. Grasses or fibrous vegetation could be used to make string (see Chapter 4, page 80).

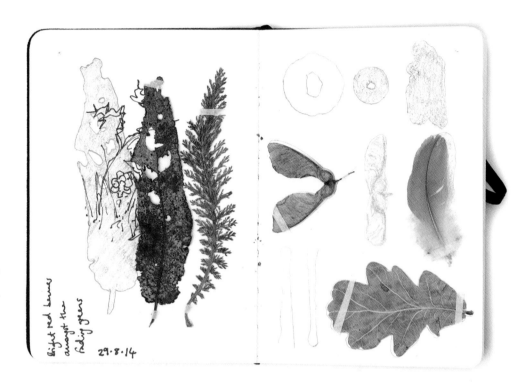

Above: Sketchbook page showing items gathered from the countryside, and the drawings made from them.

Farms

In farmyards there is often a range of metal machinery in various states of decay and rustiness. Don't go poking around without permission: always ask before investigating. There may be scope for making use of large pieces of rusty machinery on location, by wrapping and bundling fabric around them and allowing the elements to help transfer marks.

Woodland

Woods can be very rich places for collecting, especially during the autumn. As well as the obvious leaves and seeds, look out for oak galls (for dyeing or making inks). Some lichens can be used to make dye, but do not pick them because they grow particularly slowly; however, you can take some lichens from fallen branches. Whilst it is important to leave most fallen wood for the variety of organisms whose habitat includes decaying wood, small amounts can be collected for personal use.

Urban areas

Urban areas can provide surprisingly rich pickings. All manner of items are discarded and dropped, or lost from passing vehicles. On pavements and canal towpaths you can often find washers, screws, bottle tops, squashed cans or rubber bands. Car parks can be particularly fruitful for rusty metal, as vehicles shed small objects or they get dropped whilst things are being loaded and unloaded. Train stations are good for tickets and other journey-related items.

Above: Items gathered from woodland including leaves, seeds, berries and needles.

Left: Pavement-combed objects and things collected from around the home.

Home and garden

Kitchen waste can come in very useful, and it is good to get into the habit of keeping certain items. Onion skins, both white and red, store really well in a paper or cloth bag. Leave used tea bags to dry out and then empty out their contents for future use. Other food waste may not keep so well but can be used when available – for example the discarded outer leaves of red cabbage, avocado skins and stones, beetroot skins or offcuts, out-of-date spices or teas, and coffee grounds. All of these can be put to use for mark-making, dyeing, staining or painting, if you're so inclined. Resolve to make use of what is available: be opportunistic.

You can also save metal items that are finished with in the kitchen, such as food cans and bottle tops. Leave these to acquire rust: part of my garden is a sort of 'rust workshop' where I leave metal things that I want to rust, and exposure to all weathers helps this (a tray of old food cans is a permanent fixture). Many sheds or garages seem to contain collections of rusty-metal items such as screws, tools, tins, nuts and bolts. These are the kind of things that people keep just in case they might come in useful but then they get forgotten about.

Stay healthy and safe when collecting

- Look carefully for sharp edges or corners before you touch – particularly on metal and plastic objects.
- Always wash your hands as soon as possible after picking things up or handling collected objects.
- Wear gloves if appropriate.
- If necessary, wash the items before using them.
- Be aware that some plant material is potentially poisonous or harmful to human skin – always identify a plant before collecting from it.
- If in doubt about the origins or safety of an object, don't touch it!

Gifts from the Pavement

I began collecting items on daily walks in my locality: the school run, visits to the post office and the local shops. I picked up leaves, part of a tin can, an old hinge and a paper clip, amongst other things. Looking at the pavement, I noted how the tone and texture changed where wires had been put in or sections had been resurfaced. I noticed places where leaves were rotting down and leaving their own mark directly on the pavement.

I then brought all these things together in a sketchbook over a few weeks. The first layer on each page was always a rust print or a leaf print. I wetted the pages with tea, laid the items on top and left them to dry. Once dry, I removed the items to reveal their marks. Each page was treated like this in turn. I then used a roller with most of its ink removed to add texture in swathes, informed by the stripes and blocks of the pavement. (I use printmaking ink based on vegetable oil, but other inks could be used for similar effects.) Lastly, once all the ink was dry, I added small hand stitches to the pages in response to the other marks.

Stitching adds texture and subtle detail. I like the process of building up layers of marks. The whole thing grows slowly and organically. Although there is a certain amount of planning that goes into creating something like this, the outcome is unpredictable and it develops until I feel happy with the combinations that I've arrived at.

The project developed into paper-based prints with stitching and then further work on silk and cotton over the period of a year, finally resulting in a large-scale art quilt.

Below: *Gifts From the Pavement #12* (2013), 70 x 12.5cm (27½ x 5in). Paper, rust print, monotype print, screen print, collagraph print and hand stitch.

95

Learning to roam

Get to know your local area with daily or weekly walks. Explore regularly, noticing and enjoying the seasonal changes taking place. Collect items on each walk but perhaps also record the weather, thoughts you have along the way, and what you see. This can all be used to give a snapshot of a particular place and time.

Use your finds to make bundles to dye with (see eco printing, page 30) or to make marks in a journal or sketchbook. A few leaves or a handful of something could be just enough to create a record of a walk and spark off new ideas. If you bring together what you produce over a period of time, you can build up a record of the changes you experience.

Consider making work that reflects different weather conditions on a particular walk. Get to know the trees in the area so that you know where to collect useful items after a windy night (such as acorns, walnuts, oak galls, wild plums or eucalyptus leaves).

Above: Items gathered from local streets used to make prints and marks on paper and cloth.

Right: *Pavement Piece #33* (2013), 35 x 24cm (13¾ x 9½in). Silk, cotton, rust print, collagraph print and hand stitch.

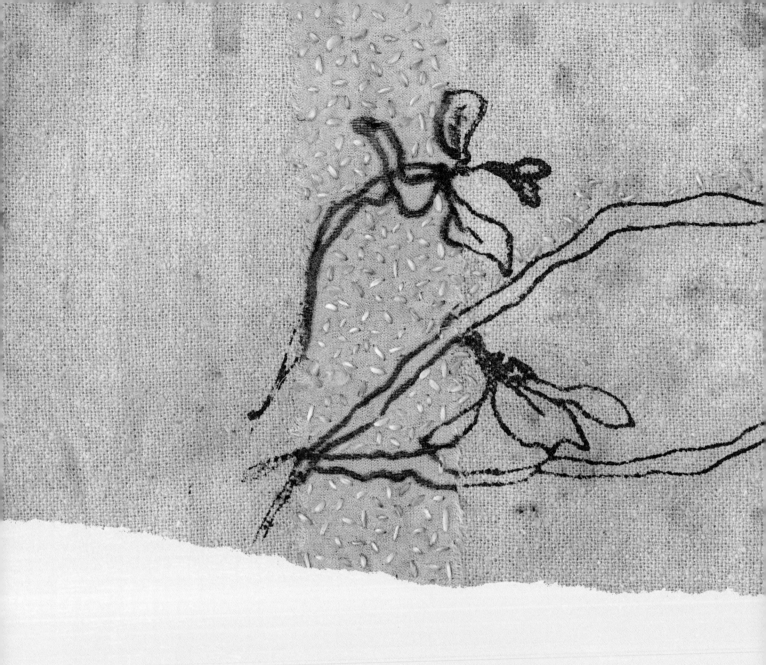

Above: *Healing Garden Apple Tree* (2013), 26 x 11cm (10 x 4in). Eco-printed silk, walnut ink and hand stitch.

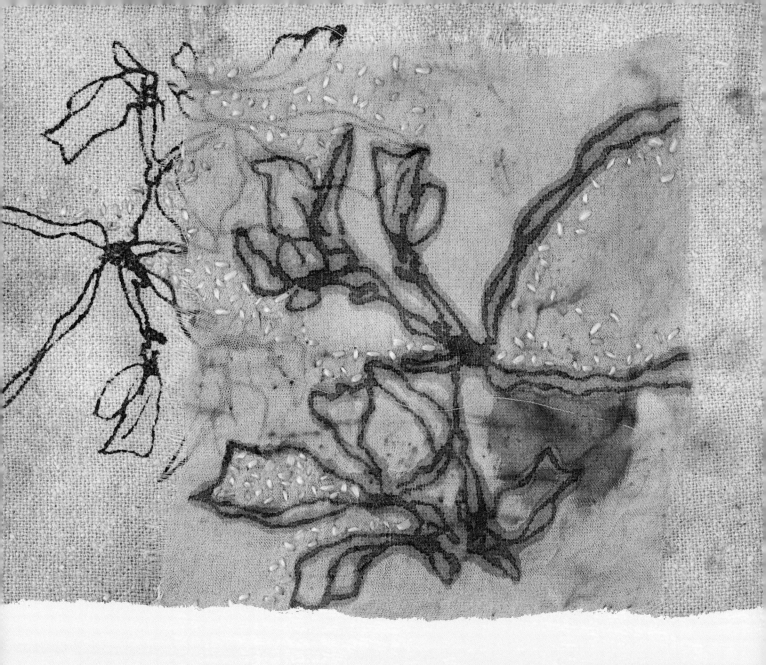

Natural colour

Eco printing

The number of people making prints on cloth and paper directly from plant material (known as eco printing, a type of contact printing) has increased in recent years. Traditional techniques have been rediscovered, refreshed, extended and popularized by a number of artists and craftspeople. Much has been written about these techniques and I don't intend to reproduce all that here. There are plenty of things to investigate if you work through the bibliography on page 126.

Australian artist India Flint is acknowledged as a leading voice in this movement and promotes a sensitive approach that recommends using what is available locally. I am very much drawn to the experimental nature of these techniques, in much the same way as I am drawn to cookery books that promote substitution of ingredients and experimentation rather than a very prescriptive approach.

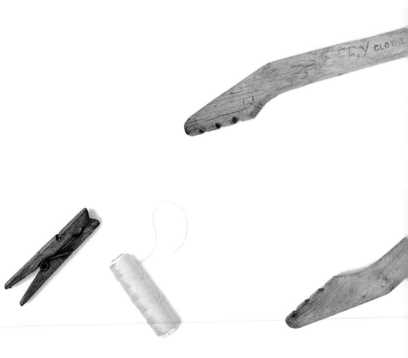

Dyes

The recipes in some natural-dyeing books can be a little daunting. However, if you want to achieve specific shades and uniformity of colour, a measured and scientific approach is necessary.

A basic understanding of the science behind the processes goes a long way. It is important to remember that even though you are using natural dyestuffs, you still need to take certain precautions in terms of handling substances and avoiding breathing in fumes, fibres or dust. It is advisable to wear gloves when handling metals and a dust mask should be worn if there are small particles of dusty residue. Always keep equipment for dyeing separate to that used for preparing food.

Above and below: Equipment useful for eco printing, including metal pots and bowls, tongs, metal clips and clamps, as well as found metals to act as co-mordants.

Process

In eco printing, colour is transferred directly from plant matter on to cloth or paper. The resulting marks can be so much more complex than an all-over colour obtained through a more conventional dyeing process. There is unpredictability to these marks: they will be different each time.

To use this method, collect a range of leaves and other plant matter. Along with other found items (metals), layer them with fabric or paper, fold or bundle up, bind or clamp, and then steam or simmer the bundle. Now leave the bundles for as long as possible before unwrapping them and drying naturally to finish the curing process. Paper needs to be left to dry fully before unpeeling the layers, otherwise it will tear. When the whole lot is unwrapped and revealed, it can be quite a magical process.

This method exploits the chemical properties of the items and no powdered chemicals are necessary; it is possible to make beautiful marks from things that are freely available wherever you are. Commercially available natural dyestuffs usually come in a dried and powdered form. This means that you can control the concentrations and quantities of colour you add to a dye bath for planned results. The use of freshly gathered material is more unpredictable but because of the contact between plant material and cloth, you can get interesting marks from a much smaller amount of dyestuff.

Mordants

Most dyes need a mordant to fix the colour to fabric. A mordant may modify the colour or tone of the dye. Commonly used mordants include iron, copper, tannins, salt, alum and vinegar. The word 'mordant' comes from a French word meaning 'to bite'. It refers to the mordant helping the dye to 'bite' or become fixed to the fibres.

If you 'cook' fabric bundles in iron, copper or aluminium pots or pans, these add an unspecified amount of mordant metal to the dye bath – in some case this will be a very small amount. It is impossible to know what the concentration of the mordant is, but it can produce some very effective and surprising results. (For conventional natural dyeing, where you are adding powdered mordants in specific amounts, use a stainless-steel or enamel dye pot, as these will not influence the outcome.) If you are not using a 'mordanting pot' as the dyeing vessel, the addition of found metals to the bundles in the form of rusty iron or copper will help the transfer of colour to cloth or paper. This is sometimes referred to as 'co-mordanting'. See also Pre-mordanting (page 41), and Making an Iron Mordant Paste (page 42).

Below: Paper folded with plant material, found metals and iron clamps ready to be 'cooked' using the eco-printing method.

Metal safety

It is important to remember that there are health and safety considerations associated with using metals and when exploiting their chemical properties as part of any natural dyeing process. The verdigris bloom produced on the surface of copper is potentially toxic if ingested, as is the corroding residue on any metals. Therefore appropriate precautions must be taken: wear gloves when handling corroded metals and a mask if there are small particles of dusty residue. Take particular care to cover up any cuts, scratches or wounds on your skin.

Fugitive colours

Many readily available natural dyes produce exciting colours. It is important to recognize that many of these stains and marks are fugitive, meaning that the colour will fade over time or in sunlight. Red cabbage, onion skins and some edible berries give lovely colours, but these are renowned for being fugitive. The addition of a mordant (see page 32) helps to stabilize some colours and allows the dyed fabric to be washed and retain the colour. However, you may want to exploit the nature of fugitive colours and embrace the changes to the marks you make.

If your eco-dyed fabrics are not going to be worn and you don't feel the need to wash them, the stability of the colours may be less of an issue. Colours are still likely to fade with time and light. If you do want to wash fabrics, wash them gently by hand. If you are making artwork that will be displayed, and therefore exposed to daylight, it is important to be aware of potential change. It is best to avoid hanging any artwork in direct sunlight.

Embracing change

India Flint (see page 36–37), whose practice includes dyeing items of clothing, promotes an approach that recognizes change. She suggests periodically re-dyeing to add more or different colours and patterns, as a way of refreshing and interacting with the garments.

Left: Eco-printed fabric book showing colours from a variety of plant material, including elderberries.

Local colour

It makes environmental sense to use what is available to you locally. Some commercially available natural dyestuffs will have been grown in far-flung parts of the world and it may be difficult to discover how ethically or sustainably they have been gathered, processed and transported. Keeping things local avoids a lot of that uncertainty. Gardens can still be home to exotic species; non-native fruits and vegetables bought in the supermarket can also be a source of plant material. Both extend the potential that is available to you.

The flora in different parts of the world has its own characteristics and intensities. Many of our native and garden plants in the UK will produce browns through to yellows and some greens. The addition of a relevant mordant will help to bring out some more unusual colours. The colours and tones achieved will differ through the seasons, so it might be interesting to test out leaves at different times of year to see how the colour palette changes.

India Flint

India Flint is based in Australia and her eco prints often feature eucalyptus. She produces wonderfully rich and intense shades of red and orange through to greens and greys using native plants. It is unrealistic to expect to get the same results as these across the other side of the world in a different climate: species that do grow successfully in different parts of the world respond differently to local growing conditions. Through her research and development of the eco-print technique, India has a deep knowledge of how best to draw beautiful marks from the plants available to her as she travels. Combining print with painting, writing, installations, sculpture and drawing, India gathers in and records her experience of the places where she lives, works or travels to.

Artist's statement

India Flint's work melds the visual and written poetics of place and memory, using ecologically sustainable contact-print processes from plants and found objects together with walking, drawing, assemblage, mending, stitch and text as a means of recoding and recording responses to landscape and story.

'I negotiate a path between installation, printing, painting, drawing, writing and sculpture – immersing myself in and paying deep attention to the environment, gathering thought and experience, imagery and marks, as well as harvesting materials for making; trying to step lightly on the land while being nourished by it. The work of each day, philosophically rooted in topophilia [the love of place], literally begins with a walk.'

Above: Eco print on silky merino by India Flint.

Animal, vegetable, mineral

The fibre of the cloth or yarn used as the base for eco printing affects the results you get. Protein fibres (basically those produced by animals, including wool and silk) naturally take up colour from plant sources more readily than cellulose- or plant-based fibres (for example cotton or linen). It is a case of opposites attract. Generally speaking, this means that you need to work harder to get colour on plant fibres and this is where the use of a mordant (see page 32) helps.

Mordants can be used in a powdered form, printed as a paste, or absorbed from the dye pot or metal included in the bundle. Some plant species impart colour very readily with no help other than moisture and heat; some don't produce any colour. Different results will be achieved during different seasons.

There is plenty of guidance available about which plants are reliable givers of colour and once you know what is available locally and try out different species, you can start to build up your own palette. One of the key challenges is finding ways to put a personal stamp on what you produce. The way you choose to add to your contact-printed marks and what you do with your eco-dyed cloth can lead to a whole range of outcomes.

A Language of Leaves

My project *A Language of Leaves* had various different strands to it, but all were held together by an appreciation and celebration of the variety of leaf shapes and properties. The starting point was fallen willow leaves that formed letter-like shapes on the pavement or suggestions of text: a language of leaves.

A series of regular walks in my neighbourhood enabled me to gather the bounty of autumn, noticing how the availability of materials changed on a weekly basis. After each walk, I made a bundle for eco printing as well as folding a strip of paper into an accordion book and clamping gathered leaves within its folds.

The route of my walks varied slightly and so I was able to gather leaves of different species; the resulting marks and tones reflect the variations. The bundles were made using pieces of linen, ramie (a type of nettle fibre) and different silks (habotai and noil), which were bound with a silk and cotton blended thread that I use regularly.

I simmered the bundles and books for an hour or so in a stainless-steel pan that I keep for this purpose, with a selection of berries and seeds collected on the walks added to the cooking juice. They were not totally submerged, and I placed foil over the top to keep the steam in. Once the heat was turned off, I left the pan untouched overnight and then allowed the bundles to dry out fully over a number of days.

Above: Silk and linen bundles with plant material and found metals, ready for simmering in a stainless-steel tray.

Right: After simmering and drying, eco-printed paper (see page 33) can be unfolded, removing metal and leaves to reveal their marks.

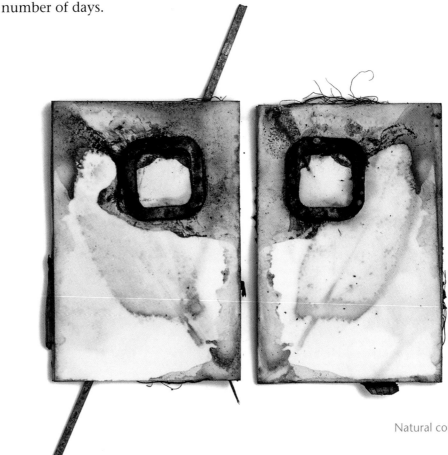

Left: *A Language of Leaves: Narratives #2* (2014), 10.5 x 344cm (4¼ x 135½in). Paper, eco print, linen and hand stitch.

Below: *A Language of Leaves: Narratives #1* (2014), 9 x 404cm (3½ x 159in). Linen, silk, ramie, eco print, screen print, walnut ink and hand stitch.

Once unwrapped (and keeping the binding thread for stitching later), I ironed the fabrics. I then overprinted some sections of the fabrics with a home-made walnut ink that had been thickened with gum arabic. (The walnuts used to make the ink were gathered locally during the same autumn. Turn to page 50 to see how I made my ink.) Once dried and ironed again, I cut the fabrics into small pieces and arranged the marks from each walk randomly along a section of a long strip of linen. Each walk follows on from the next one along the strip so that a narrative is built up, as if each walk forms its own chapter. Using the threads from each bundle for the corresponding section of the strip, I added stitches in response to the printed marks. The stitches were structural, joining the small printed pieces to the backing strip, as well as providing a further layer of marks and texture.

The concertinaed book sections were stitched together along their ends to form one long accordion book form. Again, I used the threads that were dyed as part of the bundling process to stitch the sections together. The colours, tones and marks change along the length of the book, forming a record of the leaves and objects that were collected, and also of the action of those walks.

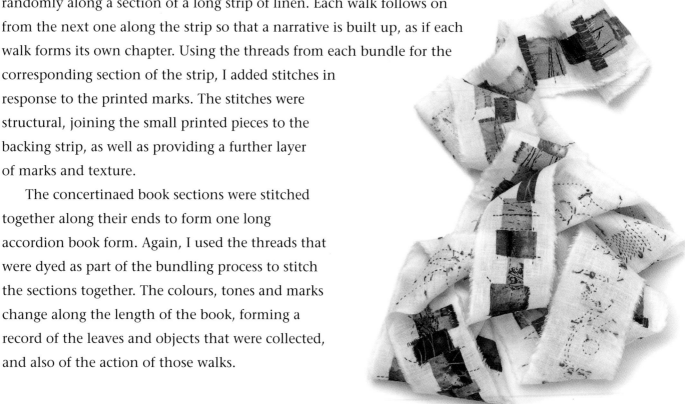

Pre-mordanting

If you want more predictable or stable results from your eco prints, consider pre-mordanting fabrics or threads in commercially available mordants. This will ensure that the fabrics are evenly ready to accept colour from the leaves they will be in contact with. I have pre-mordanted batches of threads in alum in order to make use of small amounts of plant material as it becomes available, either gathered on walks or as kitchen leftovers. These make a contrasting set of tones to threads dyed with found iron and other dyestuffs.

You can try making your own mordant solutions using found metals in watered-down vinegar or other leftover acidic liquids. It may be advisable to dilute the liquid so as not to make too strong a solution, and be aware that the chemical process may well produce small amounts of gas bubbles, so leave room in the container for some expansion and keep it in a well-ventilated place.

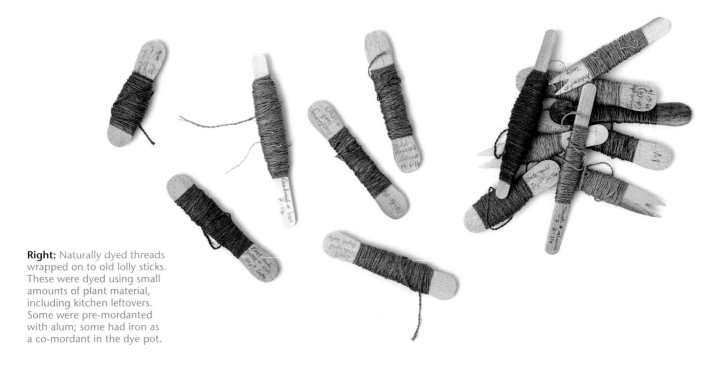

Right: Naturally dyed threads wrapped on to old lolly sticks. These were dyed using small amounts of plant material, including kitchen leftovers. Some were pre-mordanted with alum; some had iron as a co-mordant in the dye pot.

Making an iron mordant paste

It is possible to make mordant pastes for printing so that when you dye or eco-print fabric, the surface of the cloth takes colour in different ways. Pastes can be prepared using commercially available powders for very specific shades with different dyestuffs. I make a less controlled version based on a recipe learnt from Michel Garcia, an expert in natural dyeing. Michel has developed very reliable methods for printing mordants on to cellulose fabrics for natural dyeing. I have taken Michel's basic recipe but used found metal instead of powdered iron sulphate. This paste can be screen-printed, block-printed, painted or drawn on to the fabric with a nozzle-ended bottle.

I soaked rusty nails in vinegar for a week or so and this became the basis of my mordant. I thickened it with tragacanth gum, a natural gum available in a powdered form for culinary use and suitable for screen-printing. I used 100g (3½oz) tragacanth gum to approximately 100ml (3½fl oz) of mordant liquid, mixing the two using an old hand blender that I keep for studio use.

The resulting paste can be applied to fabric in whatever way you choose. Try printing with a simple block made from foam or wood, using a nozzle-ended bottle to write or draw a design, or screen-print through a thermofax screen.

Once the paste has been applied and dried it should be ironed and then dipped in a wheat bran solution. Wheat bran (available from health food shops) contains phosphates and these stabilize the metallic salts in the mordant paste. This also helps to remove the gum, which has now done its job of controlling where the mordant goes on the fabric. Put a handful of wheat bran in a bowl of lukewarm water and leave for a couple of minutes for the flakes to swell. Put the mordanted fabric in and agitate, rubbing the printed paste between your fingers for a few minutes so that it is removed. Rinse off any remaining flakes of wheat bran.

Below: Rusty bolts, screws and nails soaking in vinegar.

(You could put the wheat bran in a small cloth bag in the water so that the flakes don't get stuck to the fabric.) The fabric is now ready to dye or eco-print, or it can be dried and stored until you are ready to use it.

I tested the printed mordant using both raspberry leaves from my garden and oak leaves gathered on a walk in the woods. The leaves were bundled up in the printed fabrics and heated in a vegetable steamer kept just for studio use. Both sets of leaves gave me rich, dark colours where the mordant paste was printed, with some subtle marks where there was no mordant. It significantly changed the results I got from the eco-printed leaves, particularly on cellulose fibres (such as cotton, linen, ramie and so on).

The dye garden

Try out the plants that you have in your garden, both weeds and cultivated, for dyeing potential. Certain plant families will be more successful than others, and there are plenty of suggested plant lists for different countries and climates available on the Internet. You may decide to grow some plants with dyeing in mind, dividing off a section of the garden to give over to dye plants or just including them in your planting arrangements. Some gardens open to the public have a section dedicated to dye plants. There may well be one near you that you could visit for ideas.

Above: *Chase Devil Sutra* (2014) by Claire Wellesley-Smith. Hand stitch on wool. Threads and cloth dyed using St John's wort (or chase-devil) grown on Claire's allotment, with iron modifier made from scrap metal found at the same site.

Artist's statement

'My practice explores the capacity of textiles to carry layered social and cultural meaning. My work has focused on community-based "seed to fabric" projects, where participants explore local colour and growth cycles with outcomes associated with personal well-being and connections to community and individual histories. This is achieved through establishing and nurturing community dye-plant gardens and then through collaborative textile projects using cloth, fibres and threads coloured using these local plants.'

Claire Wellesley-Smith

On her allotment, Claire Wellesley-Smith grows many of the plants she uses to dye fabrics and threads. She also runs a community dye garden. Her approach to gathering dyestuffs goes hand in hand with an interest in researching historical links and memory of place. Claire's sensitive use of hand stitching marries the tones of locally available plants with the mindful activity of handling and stitching cloth.

Kitchen colour

A very satisfying way of achieving colour easily is to use kitchen leftovers, as long as you are aware that many of these won't necessarily be stable over time (see Fugitive Colours, page 35). Also, look in your store cupboard for sources of colour to experiment with, such as spices from distant countries.

Try everything on both cloth and paper. Some will produce different colours on different papers according to the paper's pH: red cabbage, for example, produces blues on alkaline paper and pinks on paper with an acid content. These home-made 'inks' can be used for sketchbook work. They must be used fresh as they will go mouldy if left for more than a day or so. Keep them in the fridge to extend their life a little longer.

Making vegetable inks

Try red cabbage, beetroot, onion skins (white and red will give different colours), different edible berries, or an avocado skin and stone (chop up the stone to expose more surface area). Use these seperately or in various combinations to make different colours.

Left and above right: Edible plant material from the kitchen that has potential for giving colour, including tumeric, avocado skins, berries (including elderberries), red cabbage, beetroot and onion skins.

Below: Sketchbook painting of onion skins using coloured ink made from onion skins.

1 Put the vegetable material in a pan and add enough water just to cover it. Simmer to release colour into the water (20 minutes or so should be enough).

2 Strain off the solids. These can be composted.

3 To thicken the liquid, boil it down to the right consistency. Test it at intervals on paper with a brush to find the consistency that you like.

4 Try adding vinegar (acidic) or baking soda (alkaline) to alter the pH and see if the colour changes – remember that adding more liquid will weaken the consistency and colour strength again. Depending on the pH of the paper you are drawing on, the colour may be affected. If the paper is acid-free it usually states this on the pad or packet.

5 Paint with a brush or draw with a dipping pen. Try dipping sticks or feathers in and using these as drawing tools too.

You could use ground turmeric in water to make a lovely bright yellow. Try using coffee made to different strengths for a range of shades, as well as tea and fruit teas.

Walnut and acorn inks

Above: Fleshy green walnut hulls surrounding the hard nut shell quickly blacken once bruised and exposed to the air.

Inks were traditionally made from locally sourced plant material, usually with some form of iron added to darken the ink. Oak-gall ink was the standard writing ink in Europe for over 1,400 years until the twentieth century, when new, waterproof versions were developed. Oak galls are rich in tannins, and the ink was successful because of its permanence. Traditional methods for making inks are now only used by artists or historians. (Preservation queries have been raised due to the corrosive potential of ferrous ions in oak-gall ink, but given that there are many historical manuscripts that have remained in good condition for centuries, perhaps these concerns are insignificant.)

Where I live, I commonly come across two types of oak gall: oak marble gall (often confused with 'oak apples', another type of oak gall) and acorn cup gall. These are all formed by different types of gall wasp laying their eggs in parts of the oak and causing a chemically induced distortion of the plant tissue. Acorn cup galls are higher in tannins than marble galls. Oak galls in other countries may have different tannin contents.

Walnut hulls (the outer green fleshy part, which turns black when bruised and exposed to the air) contain a substance called juglone, which is high in tannins. Walnuts are known to have anti-fungal properties, which helps with preservation, as well as good lightfastness and colour fastness.

There are lots of recipes available online for different types of home-made ink. Some are more complicated than others, and include gum arabic and iron sulphate. Distilled water is suggested, particularly for cold-process methods. I have picked out methods that are as simple as possible in order to make the best use of what is readily available. Preserving the inks can be an issue, and some people add alcohol, vinegar or cloves as preservatives. The inks are best used with dipping pens or similar drawing tools.

Making walnut ink

I have used two different methods: a hot process and a cold process (which is slow). For both processes it is advisable to wear gloves when handling the walnuts as the husks will stain your fingers – hence they make good ink!

Hot process

1 Place the walnuts (husks and all) in a large pan and cover with water.

2 Bring slowly to the boil and then simmer for a few hours. Allow room in the pan for the froth that forms and watch that it doesn't boil over – this could make a terrific mess!

3 Turn off the heat and leave to cool down (overnight is fine). Strain off all the solids through a piece of muslin and put these on the compost heap.

4 Put the liquid back in the pan and simmer very gently for a few more hours so that it reduces down and thickens.

5 It is worth testing the ink a number of times as it is cooking to see how the consistency has changed as well as the tone it will produce on the page. (I just dipped a wooden coffee stirrer into the pan and drew with it.)

6 Once the ink has reached a consistency you are happy with, cool it and bottle it.

Left: Walnut ink tests on a sketchbook page made during the cooking-down period when the ink thickens.

Cold process

1 Place the walnuts (husks and all) in a bucket and cover them with water.

2 Put the bucket in the garden with a cover over it and leave for a number of months, undisturbed. Two months may well be enough. I left mine over the winter and then didn't get round to processing it for a while longer. The walnuts will ferment and develop a manure-like smell, which becomes apparent when you come to strain it – this may put you off if the length of time doesn't!

3 Strain off the solids with a muslin cloth or similar and compost them.

4 Leave the liquid to evaporate until you have the consistency and tone you want, again putting the bucket in the garden with a cloth over it to stop things falling in. The length of time you leave it depends on your patience and the consistency you want. Test the ink at intervals by dipping a pen or stick in and drawing on paper.

5 Once ready, bring the ink to the boil for 10–20 minutes to kill any bacteria present. This will smell more than the ink made by the hot process, so do it with the window open.

6 Cool and bottle the ink.

Consistency

If you want to change the consistency of the ink you have made, boil it down in small amounts to get a thicker and darker ink, or water it down for the opposite.

Walnut ink can be thickened in order to block-print or screen-print with it. I have used both gum arabic and tragacanth gum for this. If the powder is added to the ink without additional liquid, the tone of the ink will not be affected; however, if you make up a paste first and then add your ink, it will be diluted and therefore paler. The mixing in of the gum is best done with a hand blender that is kept for studio use. Allow it to sit for a while before use to make sure the powder is fully dissolved. You will need to experiment to find the right consistency for printing; this also depends on the thickness of the ink. As with all of the processes in this book, keep records of your methods and experiments in order to understand what is happening and to reproduce effects or improve your results.

Below: Thickened walnut ink screen printed on to silk and linen fabrics.

Opposite: *Slow Writing – An Etymology of Ink* by Catherine Lewis (2010). Homemade inks and paper made using traditional methods.

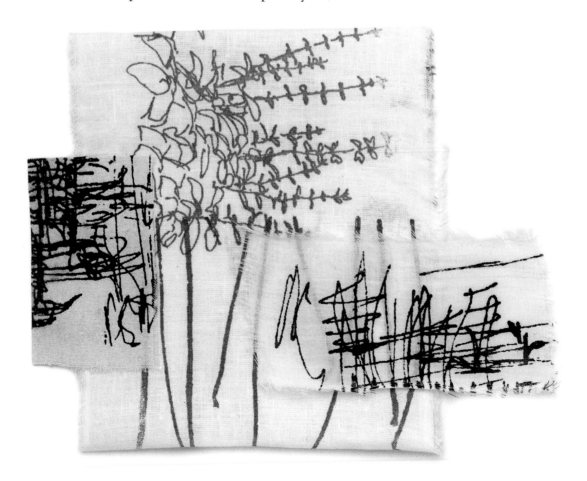

Catherine Lewis

The exploration of processes such as making your own inks can generate a much wider questioning of how we interact with our environment and the things we use every day. Artist Catherine Lewis's process-led work is about engaging with everyday objects that we often take for granted. Her project *Slow Writing – An Etymology of Ink* was conceived with the aim of creating sustainable artwork by making her own paper and inks. She explored traditional methods for both and the documentation of the process formed part of the resulting art installation.

Artist's statement

'Things in our lives are acquired very easily, without us having to think too much about provenance or consequence. In the search for ways to make sustainable artwork with only the objects and ingredients I had to hand, I embarked on a journey of making my own paper and ink for printing. The resulting five black ink samples of the *Slow Writing* project demonstrate the many complex processes involved in the making of a simple, everyday product that we may take for granted. Five samples were made: vine, lamp, hawthorn, gallo-tannic and ivory. The documentation of the process was the tracing of an act, whereby objects and thoughts became interchangeable and dialogues occurred that could not be foreseen. The collection of inks and prints highlights themes that persist within my practice: environmental sustainability, commodification and globalization, participation and process. The artwork is not an end product but a focal point around which ideas are formed and disseminated. I hope this work engages on many levels – to evoke enchantment with nature, to promote re-involvement with our environment and to invoke responsibility for our actions and decisions.'

Collecting colours

Whilst out walking, I always have a small sketchbook and a drawing pen in my pocket and I try to capture small sketches or even just words to record my experience: snippets of views, wildlife I've seen, what the weather is doing, and sounds or smells in the air. I often pick up an odd leaf, berry or twig and rub these on the pages of my book. They leave a mark on the page, and sometimes this is a surprisingly bright colour. A dandelion flower rubbed on paper gives a lovely bright yellow and many leaves give green stains. Berries may give bright colours initially, and although the stains often fade to browns eventually, these can be a pleasing way of recording place with what is available at the time.

As well as collecting colours on walks, you can use other things around you to make marks. If I find charred wood on the beach I often use it to draw with or take rubbings with. You can draw with mud, either with your fingers or with sticks or feathers. You will find a wide range of colours and tones in mud in different areas. The UK may not have the bright ochres that occur in some countries, for example, but there is still a great variation in the colours present.

A winter walk on a Norfolk beach where there had been a recent cliff fall revealed at least three different colours of clay in lumps on the beach. I used these to add colour to my sketch of the place, using my drawing pen as a starting point.

As well as rubbing earth and mud on to paper, you can apply them to other surfaces. I make small tapestry-weave sections in the studio and then rub these with clays and mud from walks in different locations. The mud sits in the textured surface of the weave and the pigments from the earth stain the neutral yarn.

Above and left: Sketchbook pages with colour applied from flowers, berries and leaves out 'in the field'.

Right: Hand-woven sample with mud applied to the surface to record a location.

Artist's statement

'My work is a map of land and memory. I am interested in the landmarks that give a sense of place and how humans mark and visualize the land. Identifying my own personal landmarks through gathering, touching and recording is how I create a sense of place. Creation of a museum of memories from the experiences of residencies in the Australian outback and the Canadian Arctic is an integral part of the process of imagining an exhibition. I brought cloth and paper to my sites, much as early explorers would bring journals and magnifying glasses. These materials were marked, coloured and rubbed with daily experiences. At the same time, found objects were preserved, transported and rearranged in patterned memory of the importance of marks to reinforce ideas that appear in the large-scale textile works.'

Above: Plant-dyed, ochre-coloured and stitched Japanese paper book by Dorothy Caldwell.

Dorothy Caldwell

Artist Dorothy Caldwell uses earth pigments to mark paper and cloth as a record of places she has experienced. As well as rubbing earth pigments on these surfaces out on location, she uses collected pigments back in the studio on textile works that have been patched and stitched, where the pigments are held by the textured surface of the cloth.

Above: Patchwork sample of rust prints using a variety of teas and different fabrics.

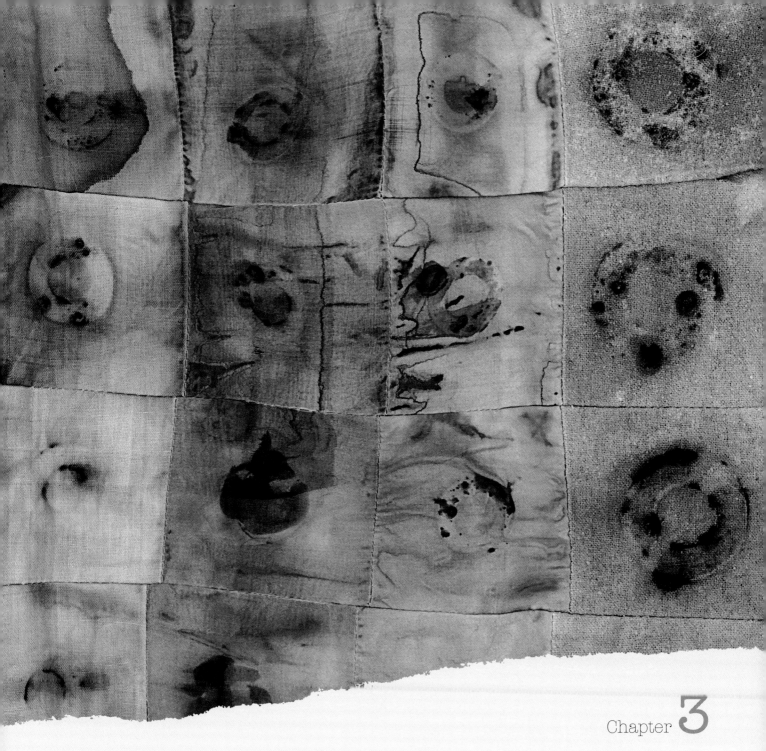

Chapter 3

Rust marks

Printing and dyeing with rust seems to be increasingly popular. Rusty metal is readily available: find it around the home, in the garden or when you are out and about. For example, there are rusting tools in my shed, the clothes pegs on my washing line have rusting metal springs, I push open a rusting gate each time I leave the house, and there are rusting bottle tops in the back lane. I pass rusty metal on building sites, in gardens and on claddings used for buildings.

I began to develop the use of rust in a project when I wanted to make colour and marks specific to a location. I couldn't gather plant material on site, so the metal that was readily available became a focus instead (I was already used to collecting found metals to use as co-mordants in eco-printing techniques). Making marks on paper and cloth as a record of a particular place is a key part of my work. Rust prints have become an established element of this, along with other layers of marks and texture gathered through different techniques.

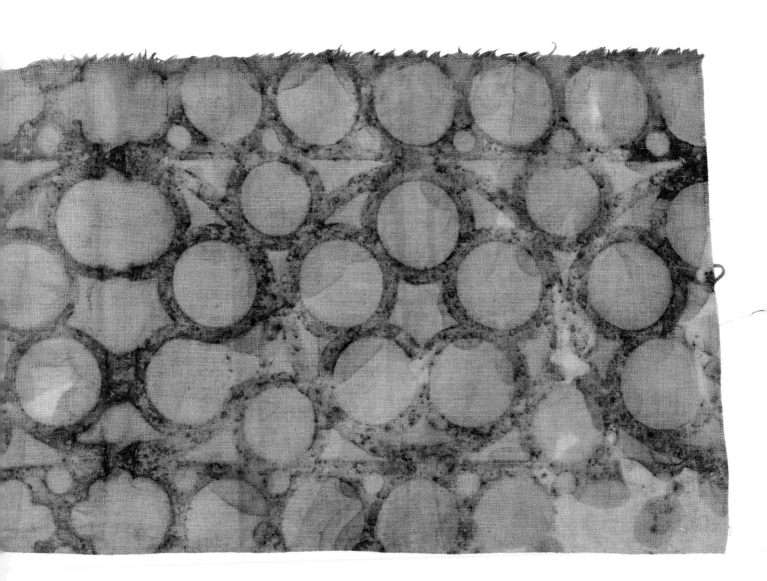

What is rust?

Rust is an iron oxide, formed when iron reacts with oxygen in the presence of water or moisture in the air. Rusting is the process of corrosion of iron and its alloys (including steel). When these metals are in contact with water and oxygen, rusting will occur and the metal will eventually break down entirely into iron oxide. Acids and salt speed up the chemical reaction, thus promoting rust formation.

Iron is a commonly used mordant for dyeing, particularly with natural dyes. Because iron binds readily with fibres, it will easily make a mark on paper or fabric: if you've ever acquired a rust stain on clothing, you'll know how difficult it is to remove! A rusty object left on any surface, especially one that is damp, will leave its mark. This property can be exploited for making marks where you do want them.

Left: Rust print on linen made using tea and heavy patterned iron work.

Right: Rust mark left behind on the surface of a car park by a rusty nut.

Left: A selection of found rusty objects.

Choosing rusty items

I use found rusty objects for my rust prints and various other processes: these scavenged 'objects' form a tangible link to the place where they were found. People often give me interesting rusty titbits and, although these are gratefully received and can be useful for workshops I run, they don't hold as much relevance for me as even the most mundane scrap of metal I've picked up myself on the street or on a beach. I never buy new metal and make it rust to use it in my work. This doesn't fit into my way of doing things.

Rust prints are one process for building up marks and textures in my work. Therefore a rust print usually forms the first layer, upon which I often add other layers of print and stitch. I have used seawater in some instances to develop marks from rusty items, but only if I am working in a coastal location that dictates or justifies the process. In my studio I use tea as the wetting agent, because the combination of the tannins in the tea with the metal has an effect on the nature of the resulting marks.

Discovering the chemistry of tea

Making successful prints with rust is not something that I was taught to do. Rather, it was a technique I stumbled upon as a result of experimenting with various natural dyeing processes. I had been using onion skins to dye paper, wool and silk, using clamps and binding to act as resists that blocked areas from the dye. The metal clamps darkened the dye significantly (they were acting as a mordant), resulting in some very dark brown, almost black, charred-looking tones.

The next step was to play with items garnered through beachcombing, including a handful of rusty nails from a coastal holiday. The sketchbook that was the focus of my experiments at the time had white pages, which I often stained with tea to give a mellower base for working on. I found that the rusty nails gave some beautifully rich, dark marks when laid on the tea-wetted pages. At this point, I didn't understand that the tea was significant in the process. After a while, I started to discover other artists using rust and was intrigued to find out more. An Internet search revealed a watch repairer using tea to remove rust from tiny cogs. The penny dropped and I finally understood that the tannic acid in tea was playing an important part in giving me the results I was so pleased with.

Left: Tea bags are readily available and their tea is rich in tannins.

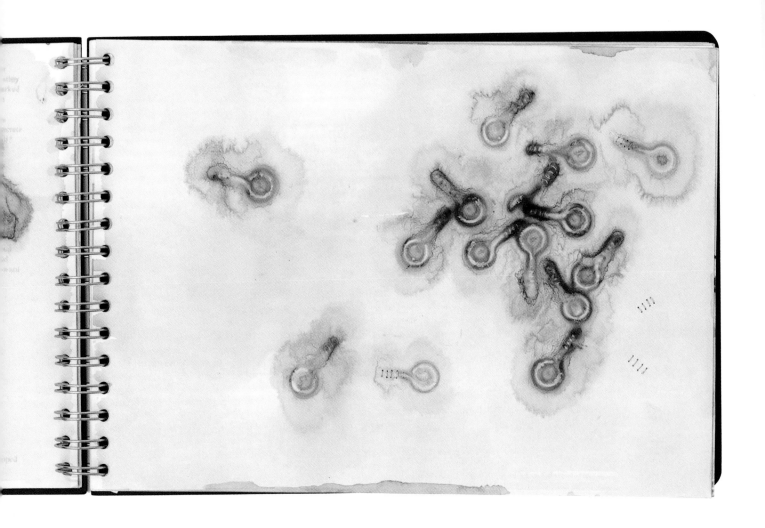

I have experimented with different wetting agents to transfer marks from rusty metal and have found that the tones I get using tea are more interesting and cover a wider range than other methods. I am constantly surprised by the subtle hues of greys, lilacs, greens and browns through to black. Tea is completely natural and doesn't have a significant smell, so I am very comfortable with using it, both in terms of safety during the process and when handling the dyed fibres.

When rusty metal interacts with tea or other liquid with tannic acid in (many plants contain different types of tannin), particularly if heated gently, a black version of iron oxide is produced. This very dark or black iron oxide is more stable than the orangey-red iron oxide produced by other wetting agents. If you are not a chemist (which I am not), the names for metals and their different states can be confusing, but it is important to understand the basics of the chemical reactions you are creating.

Above: The sketchbook in which early experiments using tea and rusty items yielded exciting results.

Vinegar as wetting agent

A web search on rust printing and dyeing will quickly reveal people using various techniques. Many use vinegar and salt to transfer dramatic orange marks on to paper and cloth. These marks are consistently orangey; they can be striking, but often lack the subtlety of those achieved using tea.

I don't use vinegar when working just with rust marks. I am not entirely comfortable with producing and handling red/orange iron oxide. Whilst I haven't experienced any problems, I have come across reports of health problems that have arisen through repeated exposure to iron oxide. If you choose to use processes that result in red iron oxide regularly, wear gloves to handle it and be prepared for the fact that once the fibres are rusted they will continue to break down and change. The Internet can be a wonderful resource but it must be remembered that most of what is posted is opinion only. It can be difficult to pick your way through the various viewpoints, and different sites are often contradictory. I always read with caution and research as widely as possible in order to get a balanced view.

Using tea and rust to make marks

As explained above, tea is my preferred wetting agent. I particularly like the range of tones it gives, from gentle ones through to very dark ones. Any tea will do, but you may find differences in tone with different types. The pH of the water will make a difference to the final result, too.

The stronger the tea, the more tannic acid will be present and therefore the stronger the effect should be. I tend to put a couple of tea bags in the paint kettle I use, add just-boiled water up to the level I want, and then let it stand to stew for a while. As the tea leaves infuse, the tea cools to a point where it is comfortable to handle if I need to do so. I find that if the tea is still warm when I start the process, I get a more interesting variation in the tones developing. Try using different types of tea: Earl Grey or Darjeeling may give different tones to standard breakfast tea. Green tea can also be very effective. You may find a particular blend or type works well for you.

Below: Patchwork sample of rust prints using a variety of teas and diferent fabrics.

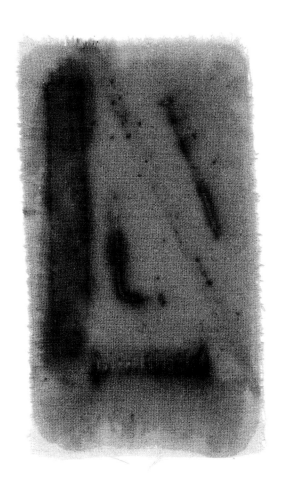

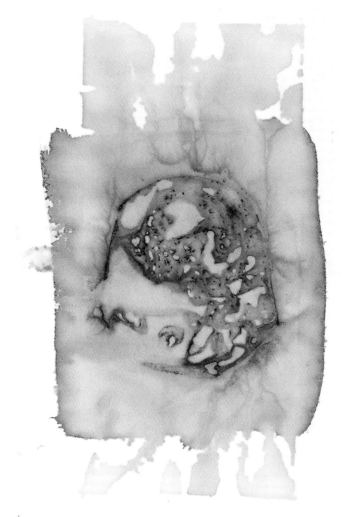

Coffee, fruit teas and fruit juices

Coffee can be used for rust prints. I find it gives a yellower background colour than tea and the rust marks tend to be very black, with fewer of the varied tones I get from tea.

Give fruit teas a go as well. As long as there is some acidity and/or tannins (which are present in a lot of woody plant species), there is the potential for varied marks. Red wine gives interesting results, with pink and purple tones through to black.

Above left: Rust print sample of found-metal objects on silk noil, using red wine as the wetting agent.

Above right: Rust print sample of a squashed rusty tin can on paper, with red wine as the wetting agent.

Time is important

With any of the wetting agents, the longer the metal and paper or fabric are damp and in contact with each other, the longer the marks have to develop in interesting ways.

The atmospheric conditions in the room where you do rust printing are important. Try to avoid anywhere too warm or in direct sunlight, as this may dry out fabric or paper before colours have time to develop. Although warmth can aid chemical reactions and get the process going at the start, things will still be happening as the temperature cools and as long as your items stay damp.

Don't let things dry out too quickly. You can re-wet paper or fabric: use a spray bottle to get a fine distribution without creating dribbles and puddles. I monitor the speed at which my paper or fabrics are drying out and often add liquid a number of times to keep it all going longer. If you are worried about everything drying out too quickly, drape plastic sheeting over the developing prints to keep moisture in.

Stability

I am often asked whether rusted fabrics will change over time. Whatever form of rust-based mark you end up with, there may be gradual changes as the metals continue to affect the fibres they are attached to. Changes may only be noticeable after many years or decades, and my experience doesn't allow me to report on those timescales. This kind of printing or dyeing can't be classed as archival quality (although the definition of how long something

Above: Suffolk puffs, or Yoyos, in calico that has been rust dyed using tea.

has to stay stable to be classed as such is unclear). Rust marks certainly weaken fibres and the more heavily they are rusted, the more extreme the weakening is likely to be. When antique textiles are found to have been weakened by residual iron on the fabric, this is known as dye rot.

I find the preoccupation we seem to have with things staying the same a little disappointing. When you're working with processes like this, I don't think you can expect things to last for hundreds of years. If we're celebrating natural processes, then change is part of that. Having said that, there is no reason why these marks won't last for a relatively long time, particularly if you care for them with the respect you would give any artwork. My work is fairly experimental and I don't mind if the nature of the fabric or dyed marks change: this is part of the life of the piece and part of a natural process of change that we are all subject to.

It is advisable not to hang any textile- or paper-based artwork in direct sunlight where it is more likely to fade. I don't generally wash my work except to rinse things if needed straight after dyeing. Because I use tea, I'm not left with a strong smell that needs washing out. I often use the creases that form during dyeing as part of the texture of the final work and these would be lost if I washed the fabric. If you want predictable results that will be stable for centuries, use conventional art products that have been developed scientifically to achieve this.

Making rust prints on paper

You can use any weight of paper, from heavy watercolour or printmaking papers through to tissue paper. Different papers absorb moisture in different ways, so you may need to adjust your method accordingly. Try a range of papers and find what works for you. Work on a surface that is protected by plastic (or can be wiped down afterwards) and where you will be able to leave prints until they dry.

Below: Rust print on paper using tea and a found rusty washer. The lines that develop as the paper dries can be complex and intricate and are always unique.

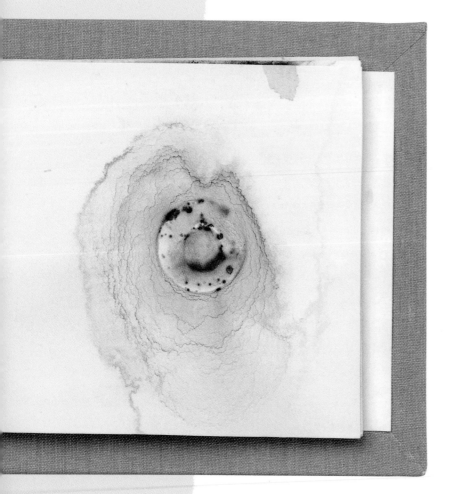

1 Brush the paper with wetting agent, being fairly generous. If you are using tea, try to use it while it is still warm.
2 Lay the rusty object on the paper.
3 Dribble on or spray on a little more wetting agent to make sure things are good and damp.
4 Leave undisturbed until completely dry (ideally a day or more for small items and a number of days for larger items). Monitor how quickly things are drying and re-wet if needed.
5 Once dry, remove the rusty items and carefully shake off any loose fragments of rust – try not to brush these away in case the marks smudge.

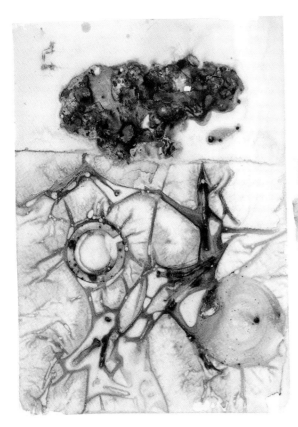

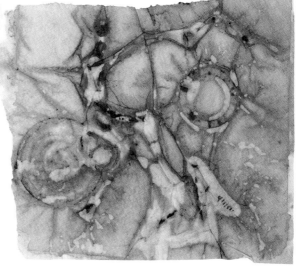

Tips

- Try to avoid disturbing the items until the paper is absolutely dry. Some of the most interesting and intricate marks form as the moisture underneath the rusty item dries out and leaves tiny lines and soft gradations of tone.

- Remember that you will only get a significant mark where the rusty item is in contact with the paper. The flatter the surface of the item, the better the contact that will be made. For example, the shaft of a screw will be lifted off the paper by its head, so only part of its length will actually touch the paper.

- Good contact is key. Some light items may need to be weighted down to achieve a good contact with the paper.

- Try laying a sheet of tissue paper over the developing print and dabbing it with wetting agent, so that it makes good contact with the rusty item and the paper around it. This helps keep moisture in for longer. It creates two prints at once and the creases in the tissue layer direct the moisture as it dries, creating additional marks that can be really effective.

Preparing fabrics for dyeing

Wash all fabrics before printing or dyeing to remove any surface treatments or other substances that might reduce absorption or receptivity to dyeing. Even fabrics sold as 'prepared for dyeing' could benefit from a wash before you use them.

You may wish to 'scour' the fabric, a process that is recommended before dyeing cloth with natural or synthetic dyes, and which promotes the most even uptake of dye. Because the mark-making processes that I am describing here do not aim to achieve even colour, I tend just to wash the fabrics in the washing machine. If in doubt, then do scour your fabrics. Scouring involves washing fabrics in the machine at 90°C (if your machine will allow) with soda ash (or washing soda) and Synthrapol (a neutral soap). Alternatively, use a large pan with enough water to cover the fabric, allowing room for manoeuvre, and simmer for an hour or so with soda ash and Synthrapol. For more detail on the scouring process, see information sources for natural dyes in the Bibliography on page 126.

Making rust prints on fabric

You can treat cloth in the same way as you would treat paper, by laying it out flat, wetting it with tea, and placing items on top. This can work better for some fabrics than others, and you will almost certainly need to re-wet a number of times to keep things from drying out before they develop the marks you want.

Unless the rusty item is very heavy, you may get a better contact between it and the fabric if you lay the cloth over it. Wet the fabric so that gravity brings the two together and the moisture holds them in contact. This method is also the best way to get a print from an item whose surface isn't completely flat, as the fabric can follow the contours of the item. If you lay a sheet of plastic loosely over the top, it will help to keep moisture in for longer.

The best way to get good contact between fabric and object is to wrap the cloth around the item and bind it; this will also keep things damp for a lot longer. This process will not give such a clear printed mark from the entire item, but will produce a more varied pattern of marks similar to the effect you would get from tie-dyeing or shibori techniques. The way that you bind the fabric will affect the marks that are made and this can be used to add variation to the results.

1 Submerge the cloth in the chosen wetting agent until it is saturated. Lift it out and squeeze out any excess liquid.

2 Wrap the wet cloth around the rusty object.

3 Bind the bundle with string or yarn as tightly as possible. The binding will help to make good contact between the metal and cloth.

4 Dab more of the wetting agent on to the bundle to make sure it is wet through. You may want to add more moisture at intervals to keep the bundle wet for longer.

5 Leave the bundle on a plastic-covered surface or in a clean, plastic cat-litter tray or similar until it has dried out. Drape plastic sheeting or a plastic bag loosely over the bundle if you need it to help keep moisture in.

6 Once fully dry, unwrap the bundle, saving the yarn for later use.

7 If the fabric is not dry when you unwrap it, hang it to dry naturally. (Rinse the fabric and yarn first if you need to remove any debris or wish to eliminate creases.)

Above: Small strips of silk and linen wrapped around rusty objects, wet with tea and left to dry out slowly. The resulting marks are varied and unique every time.

Opposite: Rust print on silk noil made using tea and a rusty metal boot reinforcement. The fabric was laid over the curved metal and re-wet a number of times to keep good contact while the marks developed.

Tips

- I often bind my bundles with a linen or silk yarn that can later be used to stitch or weave with. Whatever yarn you use will take colour from the bundle. Multi-ply yarns can be split later for sewing.
- You can wrap your bundle with dry fabric and then submerge it in the wetting agent if this is easier. Make sure that the moisture soaks all the way through the bundle. If the bundle is tightly bound, this may take a little time.
- Rinsing or washing the fabric will remove the creases that form during wrapping and binding. You may like to consider leaving the creases in and exploiting these in your work.
- It can be difficult to know when the centre of a bundle is fully dry. You will notice marks and colours developing on the surface of the bundle fairly quickly, and it can be undone at any time. However, I find that the quality and nature of the marks on the surface of the bundle can change significantly as the bundle dries fully inside. If in doubt, leave it a little longer – your results will be richer. I have left bundles developing for days or even weeks.
- You may not want the marks made by binding. If this is the case, just wrap the cloth around the object well and use the wetting agent to make good contact between the cloth and metal, smoothing it all down.
- Treat tissue paper like a fabric and wrap it around objects. A rusty food can makes interesting lined marks. Either bind with yarn or let the wetting agent stick the paper to the object. Allow the paper to dry completely before undoing it, otherwise it may tear.
- Dye threads on their own by wrapping them around a rusty item without cloth in between.

Above: Cotton and silk thread is wrapped around a rusty bolt and wet with tea, dyeing it a variety of dark tones. Once dry this is saved on an old lolly stick for use in future projects.

Different fibres

Rust will dye or mark most fibres. I prefer linen and silk but cotton and other natural fibres work well. Some synthetics will take colour, but usually not as well as natural fibres. If the base colour is light to contrast with the marks, the results will be most striking. Vintage or re-purposed fabrics can be used to make very successful rust prints. Try using fabrics with integral embroidery or lace.

Right: Rust-dyed lace and vintage fabric scraps.

Using non-rusty items

I don't use metal that isn't already rusty in my work. I like to use found items on which the action of the elements has already started to take effect. The only time I have used 'clean' metal for rust printing is in workshops where I want to get a quick effect for students to understand the process. In this case, I use wire wool to demonstrate printing on to paper and making bundles. Because wire wool has a large surface area, it reacts quickly and results can be seen in a matter of minutes. Iron filings would do a similar job. I have come across artists who have used pins in their work and then have allowed them to rust, thus marking the fabric. Even metal items such as washers that are treated to stop them rusting will rust eventually. The rusting process can be helped along with vinegar or salt and if you scratch the surface with something abrasive, that should speed it up.

A word of warning

The more heavily rusted fabric or paper is, the more difficult it is to stitch into it, and the quicker the needle is blunted. If you attempt to machine stitch into heavily rusted fabric, it could have a detrimental effect on your sewing machine, so I don't advise it. See Chapter 5 (page 104) for ideas on sewing before rust-dyeing.

If you are going to iron the fabric, it is advisable to use a cloth or paper in between the rusted fabric and the iron for protection. Ideally, you should keep a 'studio' iron just for this kind of thing, so your domestic ironing isn't contaminated with rusty residue.

Using salt waters

Above: Sea weed and rusty items laid out on silk, ready to bundle up and simmer.

Below: *Shifting Sands (Cubed)* (2011), 15 x 15cm (6 x 6in). Rust- and seaweed-dyed silk, wool felt and hand stitch.

If I am working in a coastal location and seawater is readily available, it seems fitting to make use of it. This featured in the *Textures of Spurn* project (see Chapter 6, page 118), where I dyed fabrics on the beach. Seawater can be a useful agent for dyeing, playing the role of mordant. Used for rust printing and dyeing it will result in orange rust marks, rather than the range of tones gained through using tea.

On average, seawater in the world's oceans has a salinity of about 3.5 per cent. This means that 1 litre (1¾ pints) of water contains approximately 35g (1¼ oz) of dissolved salt – that's about seven teaspoonfuls. The use of salt in strong concentrations can leave a crystalline residue on the surface of the fabric, something that can be exploited when appropriate (see the work of Debbie Lyddon on page 115). If the fabric is to be stitched after dyeing, the residue and crusty orange rust marks could present problems both in the action of stitching and for handling.

The silk used in the small, hand-stitched piece shown on the left was bundled up with seaweed and found metals on the beach, using seawater as the wetting agent. My small hand stitches were placed to preserve the creases and to respond to the marks left on the cloth by my beach finds.

Above: *Oak Leaf Line: Colour Shift* (2014), 15.5 x 8cm (6¼ x 3¼in). Oak leaves and hand stitch in naturally dyed cotton and silk thread.

Chapter 4

Foraged fibres

Threads and fibres that could be used in artwork are all around us. This chapter gives a series of starting points for how you might use collected or found fibres. These don't have to be conventional threads. Old fabrics can be re-purposed into yarn by cutting them into strips and either using them as they are or twisting them into strings. Plastic bags or papers can be treated in the same way. It could be an interesting exercise to go round your house and see how many different thread-like structures you can find or make.

Twisting and twining

The 'bast' fibres that make up linen and hemp fabrics come from stems of plants that have been processed in a particular way. Next time you are out and about, look for things that could be used as unconventional fibres. Plants growing in gardens or wild places can be manipulated and twisted into threads or strings; other stems can be made use of without such specialist preparation.

Nettles have very fibrous stems that can be stripped down and twisted into strings. Wear gloves to gather and strip them. Grasses and anything with a grass-like structure can be twisted into strings. These can then be used to weave with, couched down or crudely stitched with. They can be crocheted or coiled and stitched together to make three-dimensional forms. Remember that they will change as they dry out, shrinking a little and becoming more brittle, and the colours will fade, but they can still be very beautiful in their faded state.

The ball of grass string shown left was made over a few days during a holiday, by twisting new sections on as I collected a new handful of grasses. It formed a record of the places I walked in. I enjoyed exploring the properties of grass as a material: manipulating it, seeing what it would do and improving my technique as I went. The grass dried quickly and the fresh green in the image (left) was soon dulled (top right). Working with the grass, I found there was a sweet point where it had dried a little and so became slightly firmer. Once it dried too much, it became brittle.

Left: Grass string, freshly made by twisting into long lengths.

Above: Strings made from different grasses and soft rush.

Making string

This technique can be applied to any long, flexible material, including plant matter but also strips of fabric or paper. You may find that soaking plant material in a bowl of water before twisting will help its flexibility. For cloth strips, dampening them first may also help get a good, tight string.

Above: Strands of grass being twisted together by hand to make string.

Right: Detail of *Soft Rush Socks* (2012) by Joanne B. Kaar.

1   Take a length and bend it about a third of the way along so that two-thirds are doubled, but there is a section that extends beyond the doubled bit. I am right-handed and I hold the string in my right hand whilst twisting with my left.

2   Holding the bend in one hand, take the strand at the front and twist it towards you, then take it to the back, over the other strand.

3   Take the new front strand and twist towards you, taking it to the back.

4   Keep doing this alternate twisting towards you and then taking it to the back, shifting your holding hand along so that it supports the string just next to where you are twisting. You will start to build up a thread that should hold itself together, as the S–Z twist that you are creating stops if from unravelling.

5   When you get near to the end of the doubled section, lay in another strip so that it overlaps the short end, twisting it in so that it takes over from the first section. Keep adding in more strips in this way for as long as you want.

6   It will take a bit of practice to get it to look even, so don't be disheartened if it seems messy to start with – you'll soon find a rhythm and get the feel of the fibre that you're working with. You will also become choosy about which pieces of grass or other fibre you add next as you learn more about their properties.

7   As well as working with single strips, you can make a more chunky string or rope with bunches of grasses, which can be fresh or quite dried out. Twist them in the same way, but taking a handful of strips at a time.

Joanne B. Kaar

Textile artist Joanne B. Kaar is based in the far north of Scotland and makes work that explores the potential of materials gathered from her surroundings, encompassing traditional craft techniques used by the Scots and the Vikings. Joanne makes strings from different plant fibres, which she then manipulates into garment-like objects.

She also uses bundles of fibres in a Viking technique called 'nalbinding' or knot-less netting, where bundles of fibre are looped through one another to make a net structure; this can become three-dimensional. Joanne developed this technique through exploring the work of 'outsider artist' Angus MacPhee, known as the 'weaver of grass'.

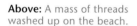

Above: A mass of threads washed up on the beach.

Above right and below: Small tapestry-woven samples incorporating different beach-combed threads and items.

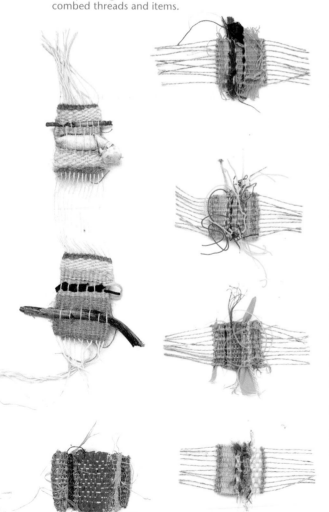

Beachcombing for weaving

I love to pick up things on a beach that I think I might be able to weave with. (We are not talking floor loom weaving here, but more experimental tapestry weaving on a simple frame.) This is a pleasing way to collect together the textures and colours found on a particular occasion. Each time, the combinations can be strikingly different.

I like the challenge of manipulating materials that are less traditionally used in textile art, such as a piece of seaweed or a crab's claw. I like to experiment with them and see how much they can be worked with. A piece of weaving presents a tightly packed situation that really tests any material. Weaving with different materials can be a good way of getting to know their properties and understanding how far you can push them. It can be frustrating when you find something that won't behave, but you will learn a lot through the process.

I have tried using found pieces of string or fishing line for the warp threads (as well as for the weft), but often I've given up after finding them to be either too weak or not able to be beaten down hard enough, as described below. If a found material is not up to the job of warp, I use a strong cotton or linen yarn to give the piece a good, solid start. I use a wooden frame, which is simply four pieces of wood fixed together and ideal for tapestry weaving on a small scale. An old picture frame or embroidery frame would do. The key is to have the tension of the warp tight and even.

Tapestry weaving on a simple frame

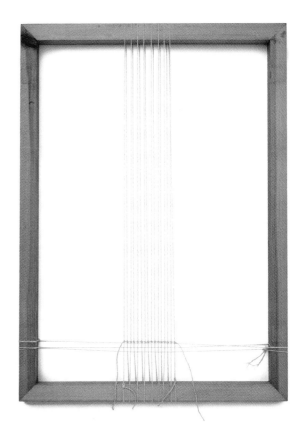

1 Tie the yarn at the bottom edge of the frame and then wind it around the frame as many times as you need and at a suitable spacing, keeping the tension even. I find that about ten threads (or ends) in about 2.5cm (1in) – that's five complete loops around the frame – is a good starting point. You'll find a scale that you're comfortable working with after a few goes.

2 Tie off the thread to complete the loops around the frame, again keeping the tension tight.

3 Tie a thread on one side of the frame near the bottom and weave it in and out of the warp threads – this stabilizes your warp.

4 Take this thread across to the opposite side of the frame and wind round a couple of times, keeping it all as tight as possible.

5 Take this same thread back through the warp the opposite way and wind again at the side it started from.

6 Thread it back through the warp a third time and then tie it off tightly on the opposite side.

7 Now, take some time to get the warp threads evenly spaced. Use a tapestry needle or bodkin to move the threads to the position you want. They should be evenly spaced and the tensioning threads you've woven at the bottom will help to keep them all in place.

8 Tie a row of knots along the bottom of the warp, keeping the spacing of the warp threads even.

9 Now you're ready to start weaving.

On a small scale like this, I use a large needle to weave sections of thread. You can also use it to pack the weave down tightly – or you could use a fork to beat the weave tight as you go. The convention, with tapestry weave, is that warp threads are completely hidden by weft threads and this is achieved by packing them down or beating as you go. If you're using unconventional threads or other materials, you may not be able to pack things down in the same way.

Above: A simple wooden frame set up with tensioned warp and a row of knots, ready to start weaving.

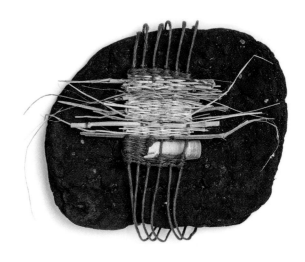

Alternatives to frames

Above: Weave incorporating beachcombed plant material and a piece of shell on a warp wrapped around a found object. As the object dried out it shrank, leaving the once-tight warp loose.

Below: Tapestry weave in naturally dyed cotton and silk thread on a warp wrapped around some driftwood.

Instead of weaving on a frame, try wrapping warp threads around an item you've collected. You may be lucky enough to find objects that form a frame themselves and so you can incorporate this as part of a finished piece, rather than removing it from the frame once completed. Or you could use a solid object, which you can wrap the warp around to weave into. Try pieces of driftwood, flat stones, small boxes or tins. You may need to anchor the warp with a nail, some tape or glue to get it started and finished, as you won't have a frame to tie on to.

It is still important to keep the tension and this may be tricky with an uneven shape. Some items collected from outdoor locations, particularly the beach, may well have a lot of moisture within them. They will dry out slowly, possibly shrinking in the process, so you may start off with a well-tensioned warp and find it becomes loose with time.

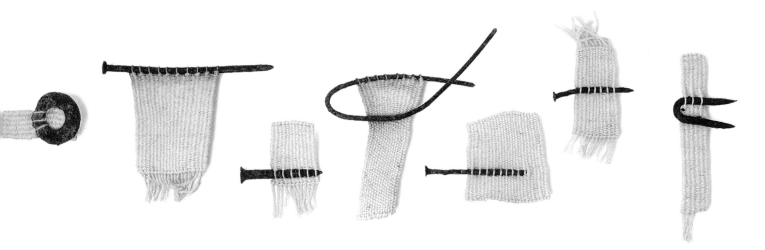

Embedding found items into weaving

An alternative to weaving entirely with found fibres is to embed a found object into an otherwise conventionally woven structure. My piece *Tide Line* illustrates this: it is a series of small tapestry-woven pieces, each incorporating a rusty metal object found on a beach. The objects were all embedded into the structure of the weave, either forming an edge around which the warp was looped, or incorporated in the weft.

Each metal object is unique and most are uneven in shape, all presenting challenges in terms of making an evenly woven or tensioned structure. Some items were quite fragile and flakes of rust came off during the process of weaving. Some had to be abandoned because the tension caused them to break up completely. Some created ripples and variation in the ridges that form during the weaving process. Some became tightly packed and others formed a looser weave, depending on how the warp could be attached or spaced. I enjoyed this unpredictable element – the objects dictated how the finished piece ended up so the weaving became a collaboration or a conversation between object and weaver.

Some warp ends were left showing in order for the piece to look a bit rough around the edges, as if tossed about in the waves. Once woven and off the frame, each piece was soaked repeatedly in seawater, as if being submerged by the tides. This repeated wetting in salty water allowed the embedded rusty metal to stain the woven cloth, spreading slowly into the threads and marrying the two elements together.

Darning acorns

As a variation on incorporating found objects into woven pieces, as described above, I made a series of small works investigating the potential of things I had picked up on walks in the woods. This started during early winter, when I was finding acorns that had fallen but were still relatively fresh, without having dried out and gone brittle. I picked up a cracked one and thought 'This needs mending'. I'd just been darning a favourite cardigan the evening before, so I had mending on the brain.

When I got home from my walk, with pockets bulging, I set about seeing if I could darn the acorn, stitching carefully into its cracked skin. It wasn't difficult to stitch, but I had to take care that the skin didn't tear where I made a hole. I made a series of stitches across the split and then wove back through them with my needle, carefully filling the space up with my darning. I used threads from one of those little mending kits that are often supplied as a courtesy in hotel rooms. Some of these had vibrant colours, which contrasted beautifully with the natural skin of the acorns.

I treated a number of acorns in the same way, some more successfully than others. I also experimented with twigs I'd collected on the same occasion, stitching sections of bark together where they'd split. I was very aware that these items would change as they subsequently dried out. This wasn't important. The process of engaging with the objects and understanding how they could be treated was the focus of my making.

Below: Broken acorns and acorn cup with hand stitch, including needle weaving or darning.

Right: Eucalyptus and oak leaves joined with hand stitch in cotton and silk thread.

Quilting leaves

During the same winter as the acorn darning, I also started a project experimenting with fallen leaves. I gathered any leaf of interest and slipped it into the sketchbook I keep in my bag. I was intrigued to find out how easy it would be to stitch into them, or stitch them together, and whether I could build up a sort of quilt structure from them. I wanted to find out if different types of leaf behaved in different ways. Some leaves are leathery; others are far more delicate. I initially used the hotel-room mending threads and also threads that I'd dyed using different plants, to tone in with the leaf colours.

I quickly found that particular varieties of leaf were more pleasing to sew into, perhaps not breaking or tearing so easily. I like to press the leaves a little before stitching into them, so that they start to dry out. I find that this makes them less likely to tear. My first experiments were with leaves that fell in the autumn. If these were too dried out, they became fragile and broke up when I stitched through them. There is a eucalyptus tree in a garden near my home, which drops odd leaves all through the year and these have lovely, jewel-like colours when they are freshly shed. I enjoy stitching into these, picking up a few each time I pass.

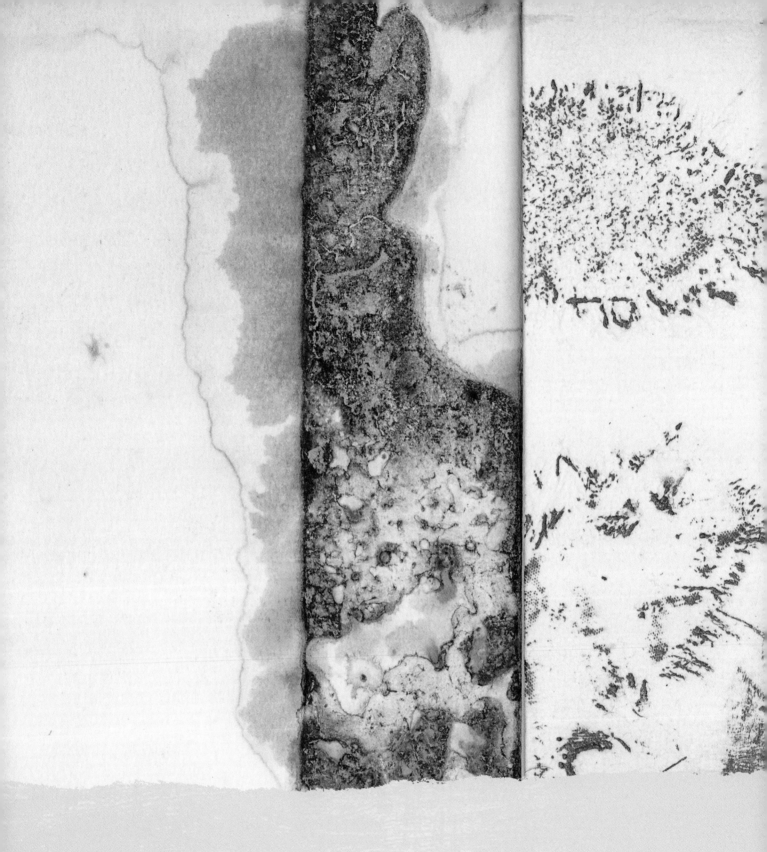

Above: Detail from *Tide Marks Book #49* (2013), 210 x 16cm (82½ x 6¼in). Paper, rust print, collagraph print and hand stitch.

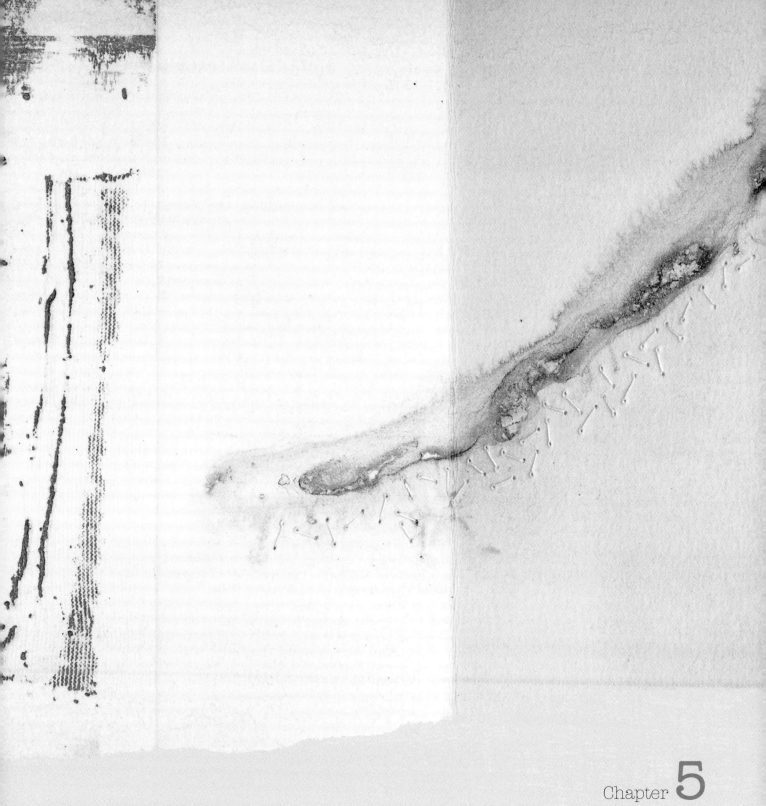

Combining techniques

Layering marks

My work is usually made up of a number of different layers of marks and textures, combining several techniques and slowly building up subtle surfaces. I work on cloth and paper fairly equally, and a build-up of layers is applicable to both. The choice of technique depends on the material I am working with and what I want to achieve. Many of the techniques described here can be used on cloth or paper and potentially on different weights of both.

The first layer might be a rust print or eco print. Over this I might make some sort of relief print, monoprint or screen print. Different elements of paper or cloth might be patched over one another. Stitch is usually the last layer, with the stitches providing structural support (holding layers or edges together), additional marks and a raised surface texture. Even very subtle stitches can add another dimension, catching the light in different ways and creating a variation in the surface detail that can really add to the complexity and interest of the work.

Below: Small sample with rust-dyed silk layers, wool felt and hand stitch.

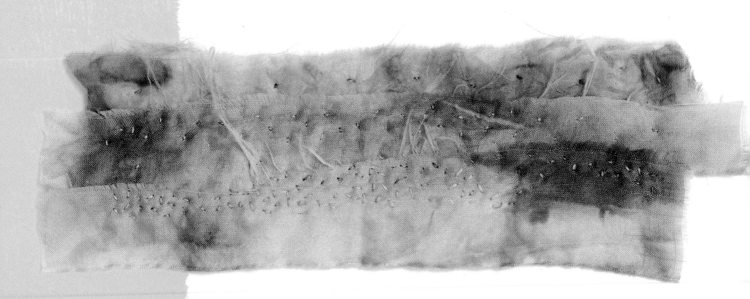

Cloth

I mentioned earlier how fabrics differ in their ability to take colour. An additional consideration is that the surface of a fabric and its texture are important in determining how successfully a piece of work might capture an atmosphere. The matt nature of silk noil and its heavily textured surface made it ideal for my *Gifts from the Pavement* pieces (see page 26), with other fine layers of rust-printed cotton gauze over the top. This work was all about capturing the nature of marks and textures on the surface of a stone pavement. The fabrics were rust-printed first, using objects found on the streets. They were then overprinted with collagraph plates, made using street finds. Textural stitches were added to give a suggestion of the gaps between paving slabs and these also tied the different elements together.

Above: *Pavement Piece #24* (2013), 37 x 20cm (14½ x 8in). Silk, cotton, wool felt, rust print, collagraph print and selective hand stitch.

Paper

The surface textures and qualities of different papers vary hugely. Layering papers in some sort of collage is a very straightforward way of achieving a textured surface and building up interest. You can mark the surface of paper without using any ink or added colour by scoring, scraping, piercing or embossing. The difference between stitching into cloth and paper is that stitch holes show up on paper, whilst they are usually lost on fabric. This can be a little daunting if you have a pristine papery surface: any mistake can't be erased. However, it can be very pleasing to stitch into paper and once you get a feel for how it reacts, your confidence will grow.

If you want your stitches to be placed exactly, it is worth punching the stitch holes from the front with a pin. You can also punch holes that are not threaded, and the edges of the holes will have different qualities on different papers. If you want raised edges, pierce from behind; for smoother holes, pierce from the front. These holes will let light through, so a piece will suddenly take on a very different feel when displayed with light directly behind it. Try standing pierced paper on a shelf with a wall behind it and then rest the same piece on a windowsill: it will look very different in the two situations.

Right: A selection of prints made from leaves using a roller to apply ink directly on to the leaf surface.

Below: Feathers are ideal for making relief prints.

Printing from a relief

Any textured surface has potential for giving an interesting printed mark. By adding a layer of ink, which sits on the raised parts of the surface only, a print can be made on paper or cloth. The textured surface could be stuck down to make a printing plate (a print produced in this way is called a collagraph; see page 97). Alternatively, you can use the same principle with objects that are not stuck down on a backing, by inking them directly. You could use leaves, feathers, open-weave fabrics, plastic items with raised designs on their surface, blocks of wood, stones, shells …

There are various ways of taking a print directly from an object or textured surface using paint, ink or thickened dye (referred to below as 'ink'). Try thickening some of the home-made inks from Chapter 2 to make prints. The most straightforward method is to brush a textured surface or object with ink and press it on to cloth or paper. Alternatively, use a roller (also known as a brayer) to add an even layer of ink. Lay paper or cloth over the object/textured surface, or place the item ink-side down on the paper or cloth you want to print. Then either use a clean roller to apply even pressure or rub with your hands to transfer the print.

Lotta Helleberg

Lotta Helleberg uses fresh leaves to make relief prints. Using a foam brush, she applies paint to the back of leaves, where the veins are more raised. Each leaf is positioned on cloth or paper, paint-side down. She covers it with tissue paper and uses a roller to press down and transfer the print.

Artist's statement

'Plant prints are like fingerprints: each unique, beautiful and magical in their own right. By collecting leaves locally I can explore and examine what is thriving in my surroundings. My work depicts the intricacy of botany and organic life by using repetition, patterns and textures. I focus on the juxtapositions of old versus new, and order versus randomness – attributes that mirror the complexity of the natural world.'

Right: *Branching Out* by Lotta Helleberg. Viburnum leaf-printed and hand-dyed vintage linen with added hand and machine stitch.

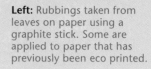

Rubbings

Taking a rubbing (also known as frottage) is such a simple technique, but can be used very successfully as a way of capturing the pattern from a raised surface. It works best using a lightweight paper or fabric. I often take rubbings from leaves, reproducing the veins on fine layers of tissue paper, which can then be layered over other marks. As a starting point, you could go round your home and see how many different textured surfaces you can take rubbings from. If you use wax-based media to take the rubbings, this will then act as a resist if you paint or dye over it. Wax pastels, a lump of solid soya wax or beeswax would be ideal.

1 Lay fine paper or fabric over a textured surface, taking care to hold it very still. Any movement will result in a blurred image.

2 Hold a wax pastel, graphite stick or other media so that a long, flat side is in contact with the area to be rubbed.

3 Rub firmly backwards and forwards, revealing the texture through the cloth or paper.

Monotypes

A monotype or monoprint is a one-off print, unlike prints made using a textured printing plate, which can be repeated. Ink is applied to a featureless printing plate, made from something such as Perspex or acetate. Some of the ink is then removed, either by drawing on the plate, or wiping it away, or by pressing on a textured item. A print is then taken from the remaining ink on the plate.

1 Spread ink on a piece of Perspex or acetate. Use a roller to achieve an even surface.

2 Press a textured surface into the ink, applying even pressure. You can lay another piece of paper over the top and then use a roller over the 'sandwich' to apply pressure to assist the process.

3 Carefully remove the spare paper (if using it) and then the textured item so that some of the ink is removed from the plate.

4 Press the plate on paper or cloth to make a print. Use the ink left on the plate to make a second print by placing cloth or paper on top and applying even pressure with a dry roller. Peel off to reveal the print. Depending on how much ink is left on the acetate, more prints can be made from the same plate, each one lighter than the one before. These are called ghost prints.

Conventionally, a printing press would be used to get a very detailed print with this method. You can achieve interesting and sometimes surprisingly detailed results without a press by using a roller as described above. A good, even pressure is key to getting a clear print.

Healing Garden

Below: Detail from *Healing Garden* (2013). Paper, eco print and monotype print.

My *Healing Garden* series used monotype printing alongside eco printing as a way of building up layered images. I was commissioned to make a record of a garden whose owners were about to move house after 20 years. This was a wonderful chance to explore a location that I already knew well but to approach it in a fresh way, looking for the mark-making and printing potential of the plants within the garden.

I gathered material over a number of visits and carried out experiments in transferring colour and marks to a range of papers and fabrics. I used eco-print techniques, and a variety of beautifully subtle tones and imprints resulted. After discussion with the clients, we decided that the most successful results were those on paper. The layering of different print techniques suited their requirement for wall-hung artwork. Gathered plant material was used in monotypes to overprint the first plant-based marks, building up layers of botanical detail that echoed the layered nature of groups of plants within the garden.

Embossing

My work often includes collagraphy. This involves making a textured printing plate using collage, and then sealing it with PVA glue followed by shellac (a type of varnish). The plate is then inked up and put through a printing press on to fabric or damp paper.

I soak the printmaking paper for a period of time before printing and then blot it, so that it remains damp during the printing process. A collagraph is a great way to take a print from a very flat found object, and because it has been stuck to a base and sealed, it can be used many times in the same form. I like to print from these plates on to paper, using very little ink or none at all. This gives an embossed effect on thick paper as the texture is pushed into the surface during printing.

It is possible to emboss from items without sticking them to a base, simply by putting them through a press on to damp paper. My *Sand Streams* series included embossing from ropes found on the beach, making marks that looked like imprints in wet sand. The embossing was done after subtle rust prints had been made. Hand stitching was added later in response to the printed and embossed marks.

Below left: Embossed sample print on damp paper using found rope.

Below right: Embossed print on paper using sycamore keys.

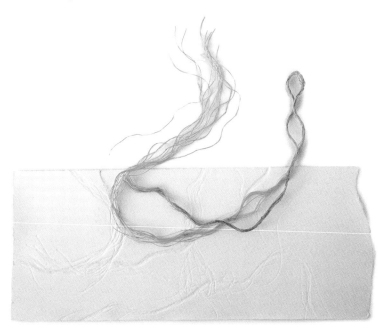

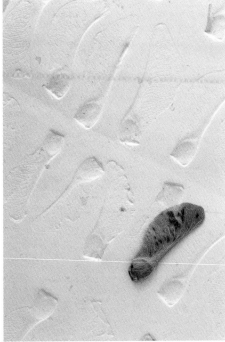

Improvised printing press

Printing presses are specialized pieces of equipment with a price tag to match. It is possible to get a similar effect without such equipment, although on a much smaller scale. A pasta maker costs a fraction of the price and works in a similar way to a printing press: there are two rollers, through which the pasta dough is forced and squeezed. Although it doesn't have the refined control over the amount of pressure that a printing press has and you are restricted on size, you can use a pasta maker to emboss from items that are not too thick.

1 For a carrier to hold the paper and object, use a piece of card folded over: an old cereal box is ideal.

2 Use thick printmaking or cartridge paper. I recommend using paper of a weight over 200gsm (120lb). You will get the best results if the paper is damp: soak it in a tray of water for ten minutes or so, then blot between pieces of thick blotting paper so that the surface of the paper is not shiny with moisture.

3 Place the paper in the card carrier with the object and feed the sandwich through the rollers of the pasta machine. It may take a few goes to get the rollers on the right setting.

4 If the item you are embossing from is too bulky, it won't feed through. If there is no mark on the paper, try a narrower gap between the rollers.

A group gathering

The Shirt Collar Project was a coming together of ten artists, instigated by UK artist Kathleen Murphy. Each participating artist was sent a vintage shirt collar and invited to respond creatively. These were in effect 'found objects', but not ones that the artists had found themselves. My contribution to the project incorporated prints taken from the deconstructed collar, both using ink and as embossed marks on thick printmaking paper and fine linen. The prints were also deconstructed and developed into a series of book forms.

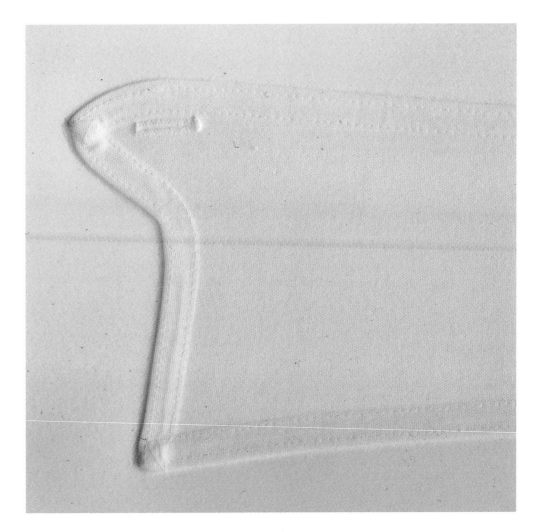

Above left: Detail from *Tide Marks Book #49* (2013), 210 x 16cm (82½ x 6¼in). This artist's book is made from paper decorated with rust print, collagraph print and hand stitch.

Right: Embossed print on thick paper using a vintage shirt collar.

Kitchen-table screen-printing

Screen-printing is a way of transferring a very detailed image to paper or cloth and can be used over or between other techniques. As with some other techniques discussed in this book, screen-printing generally requires specialist equipment. However, it can also be done in a scaled-down, simplified version in the home or studio with minimal equipment. This is an ideal way of using the thickened home-made inks or the iron mordant paste described in Chapter 2. You can buy thermofax screens in ready-made designs or order them online to feature your own design (see Resources, page 127). The design must be in black and white, but it can be very complex. The screen-printing process is ideal for textural and detailed designs. I particularly like using it if I want to incorporate text into my work.

In *Gifts from the Pavement* (see page 26), I used objects found on the streets around my home in various different printed layers. The items I found included several with text on: lists, tickets, receipts, bar codes, labels, a personal note and a child's drawing. I photographed all of these, converted the images into black and white and then sent them off to be made into a thermofax screen. I was then able to incorporate the text into my layered prints, along with all the other marks made using items from the streets.

Top: *Gifts from the Pavement #2* (2013), 70 x 12.5cm (27½ x 5in). Paper, rust print, collagraph print, monotype print and screen print.

Above left: Print made using the screen shown, over a mottled background. Fabric was folded during printing to create a break in the design.

Left: Thermofax screen with designs taken from found writing or text.

Layers of stitch

Stitch can perform a variety of different roles: it can be structural, decorative and textural. It can be used to accentuate the marks or design that you've already made on cloth or paper, or it can be added in response to those marks. Stitch could be the first layer upon which marks are made or before fabric is dyed.

Stitch can be used to attach layers or items. The stitches may be subtle and well hidden or they may be contrasting, accentuating and a real feature of the work. Stitching with 'found objects' can bring different elements together and result in some experimental or playful combinations.

Objects can be couched down, which means they are stitched over in a way that attaches them securely to the base fabric or paper. (Traditionally, couching is where small stitches in one thread are used to attach a different thread laid on the surface of the cloth, giving an unbroken line. When these threads are laid side by side to fill an area, it is called laid work.) Experiment with cross stitch, blanket stitch or feather stitch.

Leaf Lexicon is a series that forms part of *A Language of Leaves*, described in Chapter 2 (see page 38). I took prints from a variety of different gathered leaves using monotype and collagraph techniques. I cut these into sections and rearranged them to form grids of random leaf marks. Next I added stitches in response to the printed marks, sometimes filling spaces around marks and sometimes following printed lines. In some squares in the grid, I added sections of leaf, which were couched over completely, attached with small stitches, or trapped under another layer of fabric.

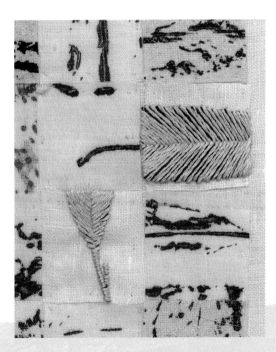

Top: *Leaf Lexicon #2* (2014), 26 x 36cm (10¼ x 14¼in). Linen, silk, monotype print, oak leaf and hand stitch.

Bottom: Detil from *Leaf Lexicon #4* (2014), 26 x 36cm (10¼ x 14¼in). Linen, silk, monotype print, collagraph print, willow leaf and hand stitch.

Experimental stitch

Be adventurous with the way you approach stitching and give some thought to how you might bring cloth, paper and object together. Here are some possible starting points for where you might take your stitches:

- Over
- Under
- To cover
- Through
- Around
- To attach
- To embellish
- To bind
- To weave
- To wrap
- To knot

Of course you don't have to use conventional threads. What happens if you use found items as your thread? Try some of the following (some could be used with a needle, some without):

- Strips of cloth, paper or plastic bags
- Sticks, stems or grasses from the garden
- Raffia or garden twine
- Wires
- Feathers

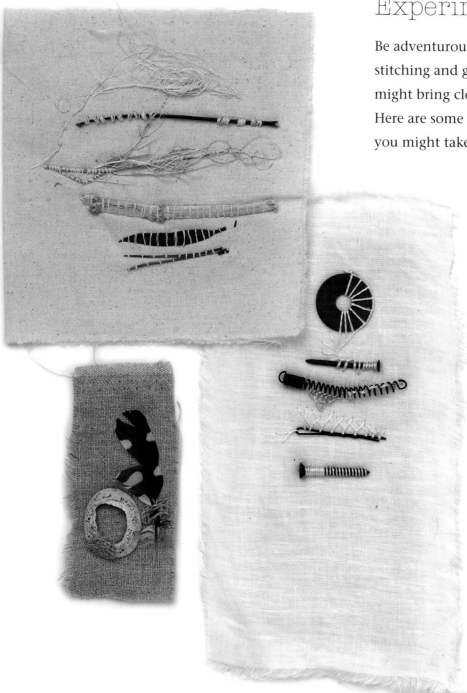

Above: Samples of stitch with various found objects including plant material, feathers, shells and small metal objects.

Right: *Mending the Wayfarer's Path* (2013) by Jennifer Coyne Qudeen. This scroll book was made using cotton, fusing, acrylic, rust print, mono print and machine stitch.

Jennifer Coyne Qudeen

American artist Jennifer Coyne Qudeen uses rust printing as a major focus in her work, but she also layers up these marks with other print techniques. She uses machine stitching to bring the layers together, ensuring that her sculptural pieces have a firm structure. The stitching also serves a role in the design, providing bold lines and sweeping elements that unite the different areas of printed marks. Her piece *Mending the Wayfarer's Path* includes direct rust printing, monoprinting, tea dyeing, fusing, painting and machine stitching.

Textural beginnings

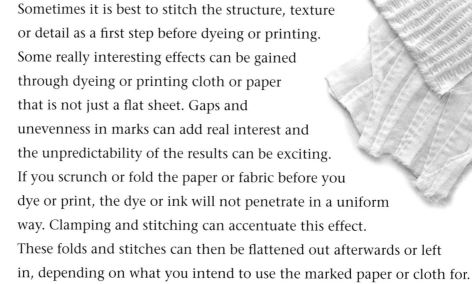

Right: Texture added to linen using heavy repeated stitching and pleats held in place with running stitch.

Below: Linen with textural pleats and stitch completed before rust printing with tea.

Sometimes it is best to stitch the structure, texture or detail as a first step before dyeing or printing. Some really interesting effects can be gained through dyeing or printing cloth or paper that is not just a flat sheet. Gaps and unevenness in marks can add real interest and the unpredictability of the results can be exciting. If you scrunch or fold the paper or fabric before you dye or print, the dye or ink will not penetrate in a uniform way. Clamping and stitching can accentuate this effect. These folds and stitches can then be flattened out afterwards or left in, depending on what you intend to use the marked paper or cloth for.

If you intend a piece of cloth to have heavy stitching or textures combined with rust printing or dyeing, you might consider doing all the stitching first. This will prevent difficulties with stitching into fabric that has rusty residue on it. It will avoid blunting of needles and keep the handling of such residues to a minimum. Working with white thread on a white ground, think about all the textural elements that you want. You could use:

- Dense raised stitching
- Knots, tufts and loose threads
- Pleats and folds stitched into place
- Traditional fabric manipulation, quilting or patchwork techniques

The textured samples shown left were manipulated and stitched first, then dipped in warm tea and spread out on rusty metal. Clamping was used in some cases to make really good contact. They were left to dry out slowly, developing rich and complex marks on the already textured surface.

Another way of working into a piece before it is dyed is to trap rusty metal between two layers of fabric and then dip it in tea. Sandwich a flattish piece of rusty metal between two pieces of fabric – a washer is a good item to

start with. Stitch around the shape so that it is held in place within the layers. Add further stitching to the surrounding cloth to bring the two layers firmly together. Dip the piece in warm tea or leave it outside, exposed to the weather, and watch marks slowly develop on the cloth.

A rust diary

A long piece (detail shown below) was stitched over a period of a few weeks, incorporating items found during that period. It forms a sort of 'rust diary'. I hung the fabric in the garden and it has remained there for a number of months, changing a little each time it rains. This is a long-term experiment, but it is interesting to see those tiny shifts develop with the passing seasons.

The second of these 'rust diaries', seen right, features different stitches that attach objects to the base linen. Many items are couched, sometimes covered and sometimes not. Others are trapped under sections of surface darning. This is where long stitches were made in one direction, forming a sort of stitched 'warp'. More stitches were made perpendicular to the 'warp', woven in and out with a needle to form a solid block of stitches. Behind this a pocket was formed, within which an item could be trapped. I hung this piece outside and the items are slowly staining their stitches and the cloth around them.

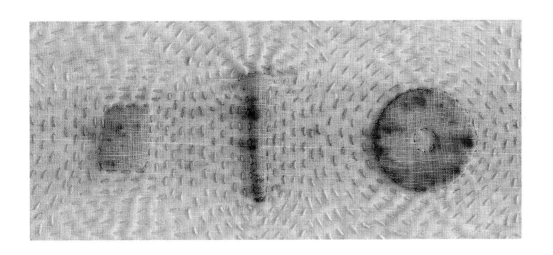

Waxed layers

When building up fine layers, it may be difficult to incorporate different elements. Fine sheets can be collaged together with glue, but an alternative is to use melted wax, combining them beautifully into a robust structure, which can then be stitched through or pierced. It is possible to trap small items such as flower petals, seeds or threads between fine layers.

As well as joining layers together, wax gives a beautiful translucency. The process is useful on thick papers or fabrics too, giving stiffness and a change in the surface quality. I prefer to use beeswax, but soya wax also works, melting at a lower temperature than beeswax.

1 You will need two pieces of baking parchment or greaseproof paper. Lay one of these sheets on an ironing board.
2 Place two layers of the fine paper to be fused on top of this.
3 If items are to be trapped within the layers of fine paper, arrange these on the surface of the bottom layer and make a sandwich. (Start with small pieces to get the hang of the process.)
4 Spread wax pellets evenly over the top. Be fairly sparing. Cover with the second sheet of greaseproof paper.
5 Use your studio iron to press the sandwiched papers gently, melting the wax and spreading it around.
6 While the paper is still warm, carefully peel back the protective greaseproof paper. If there are areas where the wax hasn't penetrated, add a little more wax and repeat the process until the layers have bonded.

The image above shows layers of eco-printed tissue paper with leaf rubbings on separate layers, all bonded together with wax. The resulting sheet was then cut up, rearranged and reheated under the iron to bond back together. Stitching was added afterwards, making a patchwork of leaf-mark layers, before folding and cutting into a simple book form.

Above: Printed, waxed and stitched paper, folded and cut to make a simple book.

Right: Detail from *Studies in Light and Landscape* (2013) by Hannah Lamb. Paper, textile, wax, eco print and plant material.

'Capturing elements
of collected plant
material, natural stains
and marks, these
pieces act as a way
of recording place
and time. Eco-print
techniques are used
to colour lightweight
papers and then wax is applied, trapping
layers of mark and surfaces. The resulting
work has a soft transparency when
illuminated.'

Hannah Lamb

Artist Hannah Lamb often uses wax to treat her
eco-printed papers and fabrics. The image above
shows a detail from *Studies in Light and Landscape*,
which incorporates paper, textile, wax, eco
printing, natural dyes and plant material.

Folding and binding

Many textile artists are interested in making handmade books, which can be an exciting way to bring together marks, print and stitch. An artist's book involves the viewer in an interactive process, a journey through and across its pages. Artwork that is mounted behind glass is separated from the viewer, whereas a book is a tactile object that can be displayed in many different ways, or folded away and then taken out to enjoy at intervals. Book forms can be incredibly sculptural and may satisfy a desire to work more three-dimensionally. There are lots of great reference books on bookmaking techniques, as well as very comprehensive instructions online for all manner of book forms.

The simplest book form is an accordion or concertina, for which a strip of paper is folded alternate ways along its length. This can either have end covers added, as in my *Tide Marks* series of books, or can be left just as a folded form. Try this using waxed paper or fabric.

Make a simple book

There are various ways to make an accordion book from a single sheet of A4- or A3-sized paper or cloth. This can be a really good way to use up a sheet of marked or printed paper or cloth when you feel the marks haven't been very successful or bold. By folding and cutting it into a simple book, small parts of the sheet are isolated on each page, with marks framed in a new way. This can reveal all sorts of detail that you might otherwise have overlooked.

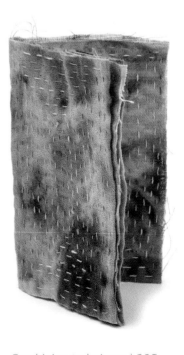

1. To make a simple book from an A4 sheet, fold it in half, bringing the two long edges together. Open out.
2. Fold in half the other way, bringing the two short edges together, and then fold again in this direction.
3. Open out: you now have a grid of eight rectangles with three fold joins across the middle. Let's call these three points A, B and C.
4. Cut between A and C (the central section, but not to either edge).
5. Holding the two ends, push together A and C, then fold to bring the two long edges together to make a sort of star. Then bring the sides round to form a simple book with two of the 'pages' becoming the cover.

The same method can be used for fabric, either stiffened or just as it is. The eco-printed book shown below right was made using a piece of dyed fabric, cut and folded into a book using the method above, and then stitched using simple running stitches on each page.

If you want a regular book shape with pages that can be written or drawn on, make a simple pamphlet with a cover made from dyed or marked fabrics or papers. Stitch the pages together with the cover using the simplest form of stitched binding. The pamphlet book shown below centre has a cover made from eco-printed and waxed paper.

Above and below left: Printed, waxed and stitched paper folded and cut to make a simple book. This book is shown folded below left.

Below centre: Pamphlet book with eco printed and waxed cover (see page 32).

Below right: Eco printed fabric book with hand-stitched pages.

Above: *Healing Garden: Fennel*
(2013), 25 x 13cm (10 x 5in).
Eco printed silk, monotype
print and selective hand stitch.

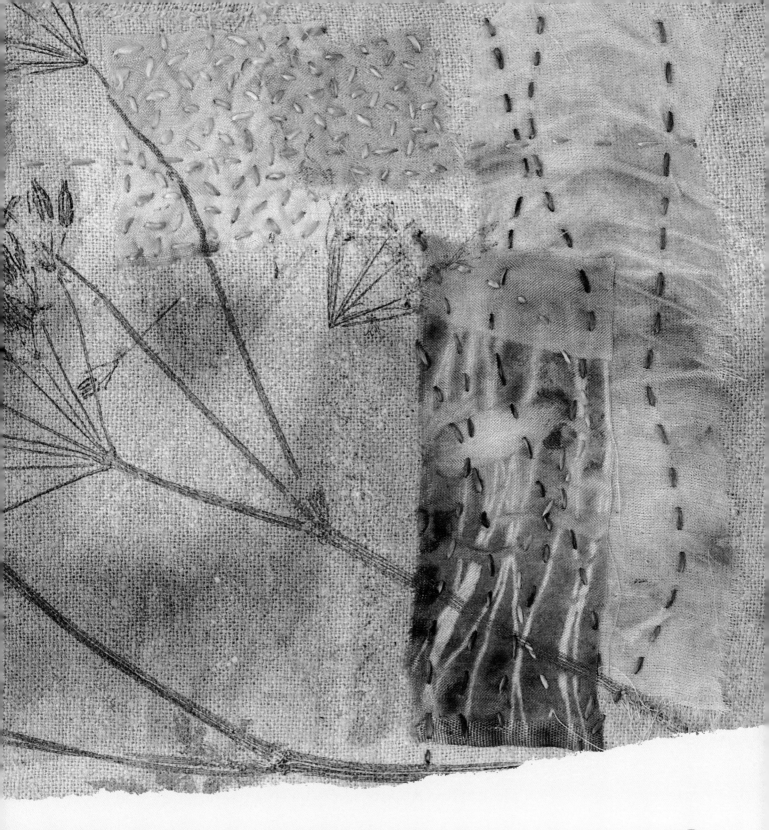

Chapter 6

A sense of place

A local perspective

Most of the artists featured in this book use the landscape and their relationship with the world around them to inform or inspire their work, recording it in a representative or abstract way. Artists often use the term 'sense of place' to describe a specific attachment or link to a place, and how that attachment might be demonstrated or interpreted. It can also refer to the elements that make a particular place special, such as its atmosphere or characteristics. This concept of locations having a special kind of character is not just a modern idea: the Romans gave us the term *genius loci*, meaning 'the pervading spirit of a place'.

By recording different features of a place through drawings, photographs or the collection of objects and then developing these starting points, artists try to capture the essence of a locality and what it means to them. If so many artists are trying to capture a 'sense of place', why aren't they all producing similar work?

Each individual's experience of a location is personal. If ten artists were to draw the same view, they would capture it in ten different ways. Your individual experience of the landscapes that you inhabit and travel through is yours alone. Each person will have a different take on a place, notice different details, or be captivated by different features.

The artist India Flint uses a term previously coined by poets and philosophers in the twentieth century, 'topophilia', meaning 'love of place', to refer to the bond between people and place, and how they interact with it. It doesn't have to refer to one specific location; it could also describe a general appreciation of the detail of different locations, understanding what makes them special and being mindful of the experience of travelling through them. There are lots of examples in this book of artists responding to their local environment, using the features and resources where they live.

Taking a local perspective like this means that you can develop a richer understanding of your area over a long period of time and appreciate the detail of the everyday.

What is landscape?

Although I am very much drawn to features of the natural world, when I use the term 'landscape' I am not just referring to natural characteristics. The features that we experience in most landscapes are a result of natural and cultural factors combined. Most of our time is spent in unnatural, manipulated environments, whether in urban or rural settings. Much of our countryside is managed in some way. But even in the starkest of urban settings, nature cannot be tamed – the weeds are always trying to push through the cracks.

Features imposed on the landscape are often a source of inspiration for artists. For example, consider how the rhythms set up by repeated objects draw our attention and provide a 'way in' to capturing a view visually – structures such as fence posts, telegraph poles, groynes on a beach, chimney pots or windows. We can celebrate the variety of marks in the landscape and the interaction of human activity with it.

My background in nature conservation means that I am particularly conscious of our impact on the landscapes we inhabit and visit. I aim for as small a footprint on the world as is possible, although there are always practical considerations to balance with ideals.

Above: Sketchbook page with sketch made on a Welsh beach using beach-combed charcoal.

A coastal perspective

Above: *Black Salt Pots* by Debbie Lyddon. Cloth, metal, thread, sea water, wax and bitumen.

Right: *Tarpaulin Cloth* by Debbie Lyddon. Prepared cloth with stitch and eyelets sitting in sea water.

Although I live inland, I am very drawn to coastal landscapes. Many of the ideas and images of coastal detail that I have been exploring, and which continue to preoccupy me, come from places visited at different times in my life. I think that we *all* have a relationship with the sea, which stems from childhood and holidays. That feeling of escape and the new possibilities that are created twice a day by the tides are concepts that appeal to us deep down. Standing on a beach and looking out across the seeming infinity of the sea can be restorative, even if the weather and water are stormy. The images and ideas I derive from a visit to the coast can sustain me creatively for months. Each experience is added to the memory bank.

However, my work is really tied to whatever place I am in at any one time. It is about *my* experience of landscape, whether that landscape is my garden and the streets around my home, the coast, or somewhere far-flung that I've travelled to. We present work in distinct 'projects', but it is really a continuum: each piece leads on to the next.

You will find that there are often links between the things that interest you and capture your imagination in different situations. The 'found object' is part of what ties things together for me. The connection with beachcombing is obvious, but collecting small items is also something I've done all my life. This extract from Robert MacFarlane's *The Wild Places* sums it up nicely:

> *For as long as I could remember, we had picked things up as we walked. Humdrum, everyday rites, practised by millions of people ... Now, though, collecting offered a way both to remember and to join up my wild places ... The objects seemed to hold my landscapes together, without binding them too tightly.*

Artist's statement

'My interest lies in the perception of natural phenomena that occur in my immediate surroundings and my current practice explores the processes of change that occur in a coastal environment. Air, wind, water, light and sound are forever shifting with continuous and infinitesimal change; my work explores these visible and invisible forces and the transformations they sustain on the landscape and the objects in it. I experiment with non-traditional materials that relate to a coastal environment such as salt, seawater, wax and bitumen, to change the natural qualities of cloth and to push the boundaries of this pliable material.'

Debbie Lyddon

Debbie Lyddon's work is based on interaction with a particular coastal landscape. She spends a great deal of time on the north Norfolk coast, on the beach and sailing small boats. Debbie often uses seawater in her work. The salty water rusts the metal that she incorporates into her cloth pieces. She often allows pieces to be in contact with it for extended periods of time so that they build up a crusty salt residue on their surface.

Sense of place: Spurn Point

During 2012 I was the artist in residence at Spurn National Nature Reserve. Spurn Point is a remote and ever-changing spit of land that protrudes into the mouth of the Humber Estuary, on the coast of East Yorkshire. There are wide horizons, windswept beaches, and an abundance of migrating birds and other wildlife. Fascinating patterns form and re-form in mud and sand as the tide constantly ebbs and flows. These are all elements that make Spurn the special place it is.

Over a six-month period, I recorded my experience of Spurn with the aim of making a series of artworks that embodied the place. The work was to be exhibited in the old lighthouse at Spurn: a heritage building that is not normally open to the public. Because Spurn is a nature reserve, it was particularly important that my activity would have no impact on the site. Therefore, I wasn't to pick any leaves or flowers, or remove anything that wasn't wave-deposited rubbish.

Sketching outside was not always possible; indeed, being out in the elements for any length of time was hard work. The lack of shelter on the beach meant a constant battering from the wind, sand and the noise of crashing waves. As a result, I developed new ways of recording my thoughts and experiences, often jotting down bursts of words and quick marks in my sketchbook to capture moments.

I found the mix of flotsam and jetsam washed up on the beach fascinating and depressing in equal measure. The quantity and range of plastic items deposited daily by the tides was surprising and intriguing. Often items were unrecognizable, having been tossed about with water and sand for long periods of time. The natural and man-made were intermingled by the elements and sometimes difficult to tell apart.

Left: *Spurn Cloth #1* (2012), 470 x 77cm (185 x 30in). Rust-dyed silk, wool felt and hand stitch; shown in the lamp room of the old lighthouse in Spurn, East Yorkshire.

There are a plethora of sea defences and other concrete structures on Spurn Point, many dating back to the Second World War. The defences are crumbling as the peninsula is subject to constant erosion and longshore drift. Parts are being washed away and redeposited all the time.

Textures of Spurn

Collecting the items that caught my magpie eye became an important part of my walks. I would pick up anything that had potential for weaving with, printing with or any rusty object that I could carry, and there were many I couldn't! I incorporated fibrous items into woven squares: one square per day, using only items collected on that occasion. Small, relatively flat items were stuck down on card to make collagraph plates. I put these through my printing press, to leave their mark on both paper and fabric.

I laid rusty items on paper wetted with tea to make prints, leaving their strange marks as the prints slowly dried. I wrapped fabric around the rusty bolts on the wooden groynes (sea defences) and left them to be submerged by the tide. When I returned a couple of weeks later, they had suffered a real pounding from the waves, taking on colour from the bolts as they endured it.

The marks that I collected through these various methods came together to form a body of work called *Textures of Spurn*. The focus of the exhibition was a pair of large-scale textile pieces, all rust-dyed with metal from the beach. I made a series of rust and collagraph prints to accompany them. These prints were presented as conventional framed pieces as well as in the form of concertinaed artist's books.

These works embody an *essence* of Spurn rather than representing it realistically. They incorporate colours and marks that are directly of the place but in their making left no impact on the site, other than reducing the amount of rubbish on the beach by a fraction. By creating large- and small-scale works in the project, I hoped to draw attention to both the grand scale *and* the detail of Spurn Point's landscape.

Below: Unwrapping rust-dyed fabric from the bolts on the groynes at Spurn, East Yorkshire.

Right: *Collecting Cards* by Dorothy Caldwell.

Further afield

With a little imagination and the right mindset, the creative interaction with the landscape we have looked at can be used in many different locations. Dorothy Caldwell (see Chapter 2, page 55) has undertaken artist residencies in both the Arctic and Australia, two extremes of climate and landscape. Yet her approach to them was similar, and these landscapes continued to feed into her work long after the residencies were complete. Dorothy's 'collecting cards' tie the two landscapes together. She carried these small cards during both her residencies, using them to collect what she calls 'fragments of place'. These included earth rubbings, small pieces of plant material and drawings. The cards, with their collections of colours, images and objects, inform larger works in the same way that a sketchbook might. They are also artworks in their own right. Brought together as a collection, they formed part of an installation in Dorothy's exhibition *Silent Ice/Deep Patience*, which documented her residencies.

Taking time

It can be exciting and stimulating to visit new places. Many people have a renewed sense of creativity when they travel, finding inspiration in new sights and different experiences. Spending time in a particular location allows you to develop a real connection with it, which can underpin creative work. Gathering images, ideas and objects from a place over a period of time allows you to see the changes that occur through the year and understand the natural processes at work. An artist's residency provides the perfect opportunity for this to happen, although such projects are usually time-limited. However, you can replicate the experience by engaging with places that are nearby all the time. Use them as the basis for a personal creative relationship with the world. A single stretch of street, a hedgerow, planted roundabout or a public park could form the foundation of a great deal of work or a period of engagement.

Take time to notice details. Look closely at things you pass by every day but never really see. This may require a conscious effort at first, but soon you will find you are noticing things that you've previously overlooked. Take a walk around the block once a week or set aside 20 minutes to sit in the garden or on the doorstep just looking. Write down or draw what is there. Make a note of the weather. What is it like being outside? What can you hear? What smells are there? What does the ground feel like under your feet? Are there changes as you walk along different sections of the path? There may be fallen leaves or seeds that crunch when you step on them. Try to be completely present in the moment. If this is new to you, writing down or drawing these observations will help you to focus on them. Sometimes it can be enriching just to take the time to *really* look.

Below: Sketchbook page with notes and marks recording things seen, experienced and found during a walk around the block.

A fresh view

The *Healing Garden* project introduced on page 96 enabled me to take a different approach to a place that I already knew well. The focus of a commission made me explore the garden with fresh eyes and interact with it in a new way. I looked for plants that would give me interesting marks on cloth and paper. I drew the garden from different angles. I spent time thinking about what it was that was special about the place, and what I wanted to capture. I asked myself what gave this garden its own particular sense of place. I gathered plants, making bundles for eco printing. I pressed flowers and leaves that could be used later for monotypes. I slowly built up a collection of items, notes and images of the place, many of which didn't end up as specific elements of the final commissioned work. However, all of these things fed into my understanding of the place and enriched my experience of it. The resulting artworks formed a record of that relationship and experience.

Last word

My aim, in writing this book, sharing my ideas and the techniques I use, was that it would encourage people to take a sensitive and more holistic approach to their creativity. By noticing details and appreciating natural processes, their timescales and change, it should be possible to find a way of working that is in tune with our surroundings. We can learn to make the most of what is available at different points of the year.

The methods I suggest do not rely on quick results and predictable outcomes. We are celebrating serendipity. The results of your experiments won't necessarily stay the same over time. Natural objects, colours and marks will continue to change, as will we – that's the way of the world. Let's not see it as a negative thing.

Perhaps engaging more consciously and creatively with the physical world can provide an antidote to our increasingly virtual lives. Recognize the potential in the everyday and you will find resources all around. An appreciation of the local helps to build a deeper understanding of the world around us. I hope that you will start to see things you wouldn't previously have noticed. Look closely and use your imagination – there are so many possibilities.

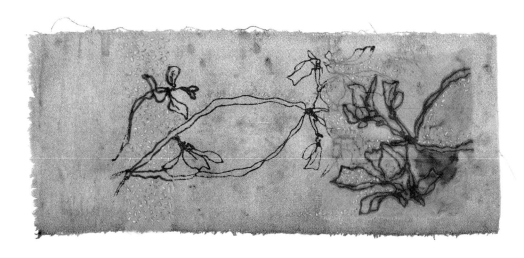

Left: *Healing Garden: Apple Tree* (2013), 26 x 11cm (10¼ x 4½in). Eco-printed silk, screen print, walnut ink and hand stitch.

Opposite: *Healing Garden: Fennel* (2013), 25 x 13cm (10 x 5in). Eco-printed silk, monotype print and selective hand stitch.

Acknowledgements

My sincere thanks go to all the artists who have contributed their inspiring work to this book, enriching it with their images and words. Thank you to Sara Impey for giving me the initial encouragement to embark on such a project. Thank you to Viv Arthur and Kevin Mead at Art Van Go and to Claire Benn and Leslie Morgan at Committed to Cloth for seeing the potential in me as a tutor and giving me the opportunities to develop my experience and skills. Those opportunities helped me build the confidence to share my work and techniques. Thanks, as always, to my family for their support. Thanks to Nigel for his unwavering belief in me as an artist.

All photography by Michael Wicks except the following: Jilly Edwards, page 19; India Flint, page 37; Claire Wellesley-Smith, page 45; Catherine Lewis, page 53; Dorothy Caldwell, pages 55 and 119; Alice Fox, pages 59, 116 and 118; Joanne B Kaar, page 81; Stacey Evans, page 93; Jennifer Coyne Qudeen, page 103; Hannah Lamb, page 107; Debbie Lyddon, page 114.

Glossary

beachcombing The activity of searching a beach or coastal strip for items of interest, use or value.

collagraphy A printing process in which a textured printing plate is made using collage on a firm base of card, wood or similar. The plate is sealed, inked up and printed using a printing press. Conventionally, the print would be made on dampened paper.

couching A sewing term used to describe attaching a thread, group of threads or another item to the surface of cloth. The thread or item is laid on the cloth and an independent thread is used to stitch over it.

darning Long stitches are made on the surface of cloth. These can then be 'woven' through with stitches that float on the surface of the cloth, detached from the material except at the edges of the darned area. This is a traditional mending technique but can be used decoratively as well.

eco printing A popular term for contact printing using plant material to make marks on cloth and paper. The plant material is wrapped or layered and bound between cloth or paper, with or without pre-mordanting or co-mordant ingredients. The 'bundle' is then steamed, simmered or composted to facilitate the transfer of plant pigments to the cloth or paper. This technique is based on natural dyeing traditions but can reveal colours that differ from immersion techniques.

flotsam The floating wreckage of a ship or its cargo, often washed up on beaches and available to beachcombers.

foraging The act of looking for, or searching for, materials of use, usually in a natural or wild setting.

gsm Grams per square metre. The conventional way to label weight of paper used for art techniques.

gum arabic Gum from the dried sap of certain acacia trees, grown and produced in parts of Africa and the Middle East. Used in the food industry as a stabilizer and as a binder in the preparation of art materials.

jetsam Part of a ship's cargo that has purposefully been thrown overboard. Often washed up on beaches, where it is available to beachcombers.

monoprint or monotype A fine-art printmaking term referring to a print that is a one-off rather than one that is reproduced a number of times. It is made using a featureless plate as a base, which is inked or painted in an expressive way.

mordant A substance used to help a dyestuff to adhere to fibres, often modifying the colour or tone of the dye. Commonly used mordants include iron, copper, tannins, salt, alum and vinegar.

needle weaving An embroidery technique that would traditionally be done as part of drawn thread work. Using a needle, a thread is woven backwards and forwards, forming a 'weft' around threads that are part of the structure of the base cloth. This is similar to surface darning, but uses the base cloth rather than added stitches as its basis.

printing plate A surface from which a print is taken, usually using a printing press. This can be metal, wood, card or plastic. A printing plate can be textured (for example a collagraph plate) or smooth (as in monotype printing).

ramie Fabric made from the bast (stem) fibres of an East Asian plant from the nettle family. Similar to linen.

relief printing Ink is applied to a textured plate or object, usually with a roller, so that the raised relief takes ink but the areas between do not. A print is taken from this using a printing press or using a roller or brayer to make firm contact.

shibori Techniques traditional to Japan, using stitching, clamping or folding as a resist to dye.

scavenge To search for and collect anything of use from items that have previously been discarded.

silk habotai A plain-weave silk fabric that is lightweight and easy to dye.

silk noil Silk fabric made from the short fibres left over from spinning silk that is textured and matt.

Synthrapol A neutral soap, used for the scouring process before dyeing.

tapestry weave An interlaced structure of warp (vertical) and weft (horizontal) threads, where the warp is usually completely covered by the weft.

thermofax screen For screen printing designs on to fabric (see Resources, page 127).

tragacanth gum Gum from the dried sap of plants of the Astragalus genus. Mostly grown and produced in the Middle East. Used as a binder for artist's pastels and for pharmaceutical and culinary uses.

warp The vertical threads of a woven structure, held under tension on a frame or loom during weaving.

weft The horizontal threads of a woven structure, threaded in and out of the warp threads.

Bibliography

Benn, Claire, Jane Dunnewold, and Leslie Morgan. *Finding Your Own Visual Language: A Practical Guide to Design and Composition* (Committed to Cloth, 2007).

Bevan, Jane. *Craft from Natural Materials* (Bloomsbury, 2013).

Brockie, Keith, *Keith Brockie's Wildlife Sketchbook* (J. M. Dent, 1981).

Buckland, David, *Burning Ice: Art and Climate Change* (Cape Farewell, 2006).

Buckland, David, and Chris Wainwright (eds.), *Unfold: A Cultural Response to Climate Change* (Springer, 2010).

Cane, Kyra, *Making and Drawing* (Bloomsbury, 2012).

Court, Sibella, *Bowerbird* (Hardie Grant, 2012).

Crook, Jackie, *Natural Dyeing* (Gaia Books, 2007).

Dean, Jenny, *The Craft of Natural Dyeing* (Search Press, 1994).

Decker, Julie, *Gyre: The Plastic Ocean* (Booth-Clibborn Editions, 2014).

Drury, Chris, *Found Moments in Time and Space* (Harry N. Abrams, 1998).

Edwards, Betty, *Drawing on the Right Side of the Brain* (Harper Collins, 2001).

Farley, Paul, and Michael Symmons Roberts, *Edgelands: Journeys into England's True Wilderness* (Vintage, 2012).

Flint, India, *Eco Colour* (Murdoch Books, 2008).

Flint, India, *Second Skin* (Murdoch Books, 2011).

Franck, Frederick, *Zen Seeing, Zen Drawing* (Bantam Books, 1993).

Goldsworthy, Andy, *Andy Goldsworthy* (Viking, 1990).

Gooding, Mel, *Song of the Earth* (Thames & Hudson, 2002).

Greenlees, Kay, *Creating Sketchbooks for Embroiderers and Textile Artists* (Batsford, 2005).

Holmes, Cas, *The Found Object in Textile Art* (Batsford, 2010).

Howard, Sarah, and Elisabeth Kendrick, *Creative Weaving* (Gaia Books, 2007).

MacFarlane, Robert, *The Wild Places* (Granta Publications, 2007).

Neddo, Nick, *The Organic Artist* (Quarry Books, 2015)

Rivers, Charlotte, *Little Book of Book Making* (Potter Craft, 2014).

Singer, Ruth, *Sew Eco* (A. & C. Black, 2010).

Solnit, Rebecca, *Wanderlust: A History of Walking* (Verso, 2001).

Soroka, Joanne, *Tapestry Weaving: Design and Technique* (Crowood, 2011)

Taylor, Terry, *Eco Books* (Lark Books, 2009).

Tellier-Loumagne, Françoise, *The Art of Embroidery* (Thames & Hudson, 2006).

Thomas, Mary, *Mary Thomas's Embroidery Book* (Hodder & Stoughton, 1936).

Tufnell, Ben, *Land Art* (Tate Publishing, 2006).

Wallis, Clarrie, *Richard Long: Heaven and Earth* (Tate Publishing, 2009).

Wolf, Collette, *The Art of Manipulating Fabric* (Krause Publications, 1996).

Resources

A group gathering: the Shirt Collar Project
www.agroupgathering.blogspot.co.uk

Art Van Go – suppliers of materials for fine art
and textile art
www.artvango.co.uk

Catherine Lewis – artist
www.catlewis.com

Claire Wellesley-Smith – artist
www.clairewellesleysmith.co.uk

Debbie Lyddon – artist
www.debbielyddon.co.uk

Dorothy Caldwell – artist
www.dorothycaldwell.com

Good Beach Guide
www.goodbeachguide.co.uk

Green Fibres – organic and fair-trade fabrics
www.greenfibres.com

Growing Colour – dye garden blog
www.growingcolour.blogspot.co.uk

Habu – unusual yarns
www.habutextiles.com

Hannah Lamb – artist
www.hannahlamb.co.uk

House of Hemp – hemp yarns
www.houseofhemp.co.uk

India Flint – artist and natural dye expert
www.indiaflint.com

Jennifer Coyne Qudeen – artist
www.jennifercoynequdeen.blogspot.co.uk

Jilly Edwards – tapestry weaver
www.jillyedwards.co.uk

Joanne B. Kaar – artist
www.joannebkaar.com

Lotta Helleberg – artist
www.lottahelleberg.com

Marine Conservation Society – beach-cleaning events
www.mcsuk.org/beachwatch

Michel Garcia – natural dye expert
www.michelgarcia.fr

Permacouture – sustainable fashion and textiles
organization
www.permacouture.org

The Sketchbook Project
www.thesketchbookproject.com

Slow Movement
www.slowmovement.com

Sue Lawty – artist
www.suelawty.co.uk

Thermofax Screens
www.thermofaxscreens.co.uk

Threadborne – eco printing and natural dyeing blog
www.wendyfe.wordpress.com

Wild Colour – Jenny Dean, natural dye expert
www.jennydean.co.uk

Wildlife Trusts – nature reserves to visit. Some wildlife
trusts also hold beach-cleaning events.
www.wildlifetrusts.org

Index

Alice Fox is an embroiderer and textile artist who has a strong interest in the natural world. Her practice brings together recording, collecting and interaction with the landscape. In 2012 she was artist-in-residence at Spurn Point National Nature Reserve in East Yorkshire, an experience that has informed much of her recent work.